Indian Railways
Strategy for Reforms

K. B. Verma

FOUNDATION
BOOKS

FOUNDATION
BOOKS

Foundation Books is an imprint of Cambridge University Press, India

Cambridge House, 4381/4 Ansari Road, Daryaganj, New Delhi 110 002

www.cambridgeindia.org

First published 2015

Printed in India at Sanat Printers, Kundli, Haryana

ISBN 978-93-84463-15-1 Paperback

In memory of
my mother Shanti whom I lost when less than four

Contents

List of Tables and Charts

Tables

Charts

Preface

This book is a sequel to my paper titled 'In Pursuit of a Productive Relationship' for a seminar on 'Management of Change in Railway Business' organised jointly by the International Union of Railways (UIC) and Indian Railways in November 1990 in Delhi. The paper basically dealt with the relationship between Indian Railways and the Government of India. It only concretised the issues involved. It did not offer any suggestions except that since this subject has never been really examined, except in passing by a couple of committees, there was an urgent need to have it examined in depth as a single term of reference by a committee of experts. A single term reference is required because of the complexities and all-round sensitivities involved in such an exercise – particularly in view of the changed economic environment, the developments in the transport sector and the role which can be played by Railways in the economic and social lives of the people. Unfortunately, neither any such committee has been set up nor has the issue been examined by any expert in as much detail as called for. 'The Expert Group on Indian Railways: Indian Railway Report: Policy Imperatives for Reinvention and Growth' popularly known as the Rakesh Mohan Committee Report (2001) did touch upon it. But in a limited way. Perhaps because like other committees on Indian Railways, it dealt with many other issues. And like so many other recommendations of so many other committees, the recommendations of the Rakesh Mohan Committee too were put on the back burner.

My tenure with Indian Railways in various capacities in the Accounts department as a member of the Indian Railway Accounts Service, a stint on a generalist's post as Additional Divisional Railway Manager in one of the larger Divisions of the Railways, teaching assignment with the Railway Staff College (now National Academy of Indian Railways), Vadodara which is the apex training institute for officers of Indian Railways, assignments with Rites which is a consultancy company of Indian Railways and IRCON which is a construction company of Indian Railways as well as couple of assignments abroad gave me unique opportunities to look at Indian Railways from different angles, both as an insider and as an outsider. The credit for shaping the ideas presented in this book must go to them.

This book is not confined to state railway relationship. Railways' problems are not unidimensional. They are multidimensional. However, this book tries to deal with only one issue, i.e., what needs to be done to reform Indian Railways with minimum upheaval.

Reform is also not unidimensional. Consequently, most of the measures suggested in this book are interconnected and interdependent. The success of one depends upon the implementation of the other. For example, commercialisation of Indian Railways cannot be imagined without according primacy to the commercial function. And corporatisation and commercialisation of Indian Railways would be ineffective without independent Members from industry and financial sectors on the Board.

I have tried to bring together suggestions made by various railway experts and committees on Indian Railways as well as some of my own ideas such as primacy to the commercial function, creation of an Indian Railway Executive Service, selection for the posts of Chairman Railway Board, Members of the Railway Board and General Managers of zonal railways to be made by the Union Public Service Commission or the Public Enterprises Selection Board, induction of Independent Members from the industrial and banking sectors into the Railway Board, modifying the Productivity Linked Bonus scheme to include both physical and financial parameters in order to make it work as a proper incentive scheme, extending the incentive scheme to all categories of employees, professionalising the non-professional functions and so on. Effort has been made to develop a holistic structure as a piecemeal approach is highly unlikely to succeed.

The book is divided into three parts: Part 1 introduces the reader to Indian Railways. Those who are familiar with Indian Railways may skip it without much loss. But in their case also, it may help to refresh their memory. Besides basic facts about Indian Railways, it includes a very brief historical evolution of the current financial structures in order to put things in proper perspective. The observations and recommendations of the Acworth Committee, 1921 are rather interesting and appear to be as of today. There is also a brief chapter on the performance of Indian Railways which provides the rationale for reforms.

Part 2 deals with reforms in some foreign railways. It is seen that the reasons forcing the governments to reform their railways, the philosophy of reform and the basic features of the reform were remarkably similar in all countries. They differed only in the structures created by them – and they differed widely. Each response was shaped by local circumstances as well as political compulsions. In case of the United Kingdom it was idealism plus financial problem. Thatcherism was as much responsible for reforms as the need to cut down on subsidies provided to British Rail. Of the many railways where reforms have been carried out, the structure of reforms in three railways viz. Japanese Railways, Swedish Railways and British Railways have been covered in some detail as they bring out the essentials of the business models which are now emerging in the railway world. The reforms in Russian Railways and German Railways have also been described but only briefly as they basically follow the Swedish model. Reforms in Chinese Railways are in early stages and have just appeared on the horizon.

Part 1 and Part 2 serve as a background to Part 3 which is the heart of the book.

Chapter 9 describes the strategy for reforms for Indian Railways. It provides the rationale for the type and characteristics of the suggested reform measures, so to say the philosophy of reforms. Needless to say, the underlying philosophy of any reform will depend on what is sought to be achieved by it. It is seen from the experience in other countries that the essence of railway reforms lay in the creation of a structure which enabled self-sustained motivation to improve and grow. This has to be the mantra for Indian Railways too. It is a different matter that they came up with different responses depending on local conditions.

In this book, the proposed strategy for Indian Railways is based on the belief that there is nothing fundamentally wrong with the existing structure of Indian Railways except for two – excessive external control and lack of commercial orientation. Actually, the two also boil down to one, viz. commercial orientation. It is these two issues which need to be addressed. But for this to be achieved, it is contended that the drastic structural changes carried out by other Railways are not really required in Indian Railways. In fact, they would not only be unworkable, but also catastrophic. What is required is creation of appropriate institutions and appropriate systems. Once this is done, other improvements will follow. The compulsions of the reformed structure itself will compel other reforms and improvements which will, more likely than not, become self-sustaining.

The proposals for reform are covered from Chapter 10 to 14. Chapter 15 tries to put them together in a structural whole and evaluate the model from the point of view of practicability, the pitfalls and the conditions necessary for its success. A possible stage-wise approach is given in Chapter 16.

Most of the suggestions are bound to create controversy. As long as they do so, they serve the purpose and are welcome. As the saying goes – thesis, antithesis and synthesis. Informed debates are healthy. They give rise to innovative ideas, provided they are not burdened with preconceived notions, prejudices, biases, fear of the unknown and lack of courage to change. They generate more heat than light.

One of the most controversial issues will be those dealt with in Chapter 11 on the Management Structure and Chapter 12 on the Incentive Scheme.

Some of the suggestions may appear rather cataclysmic in comparison with what exists in Indian Railways today. But they are nothing more than mild tremors in comparison to what has been done in many other railways.

It is true that in almost all countries, the reform process was initiated by the government. In Sweden, it was the railway management which was instrumental in pushing the government towards reform, though more to protect its own turf than for purely altruistic reasons. Can the Indian Railways management push for the reforms or at least implement those measures which are within its area of competence or least likely to be resisted? Perhaps the fleetingly short tenures at the highest echelons of management strongly militate against such a prospect.

Having described what this book is about, it is important to clarify what it is 'not about'. It is not about ways and means to increase revenues, cut costs, improve investment decisions, generate funds for investment etc. As mentioned above, it is believed that after the reform measures are implemented, the compulsions of a commercial entity buttressed by human nature will, on their own, lead to more and more innovative ways to achieve the above-mentioned very important objectives.

Though by no means comprehensive, it is hoped that this book in some way contributes to denting some long-held beliefs and in convincing the powers that be reform in Indian Railways is much overdue, beneficial to all and that it is not too difficult.

A word of apology is owed to the readers. The Railway Budget for 2014–15 has been presented to the Parliament on 8 July 2014 when this book was in almost last stages of printing. The figures quoted in this book are, therefore, out of date by one year. But since the subject is very topical it was considered advisable to go ahead with its printing rather than delay it by revising the figures. However, the essentials of the book in no way get compromised.

One more point. For the fist time in recent memory, this year's budget has taken a first step towards reforming Indian Railways. It has been decided to separate the two functions of policy formulation and implementation in the Railway Board. Details are not yet available. Hence it is not possible to examine its contours. But though welcome, it is only a very tiny and inadequate step. Unless it is accompanied by other measures, it may turn out to be nothing more than cosmetic.

I acknowledge with gratitude the comments and advice from Sri M. Ravindra, Former Chairman Railway Board and ex-officio Principal Secretary to the Government of India and Sri Shanti Narain, Former Member Traffic, Railway Board and ex-officio Secretary to the Government of India. Sri Ravindra was also a Member of the Rakesh Mohan Committee. I benefited immensely from them. But the responsibility for the contents of this book must remain entirely mine.

Finally, I thank my wife Abha for bearing with me during my long hours of research and writing of this book.

New Delhi

K.B. Verma

List of Abbreviations

ADRM	Additional Divisional Railway Manager
ASSOCHAM	Association of Chambers of Commerce
BR	British Rail
BV	Ban Verket
CCI	Cabinet Committee on Investments
CII	Chamber of Indian Industries
COFMOW	Centre for Modernisation of Workshops
CMD	Chairman cum Managing Director
CONCOR	Container Corporation of India Ltd
CPTA	County Transport Authority
CR	Central Railway
Cr.	Crore i.e., 10 million
CRB	Chairman Railway Board
CRC	Chinese Railway Corporation
CTC	Cost to Company
DB	Deutsche Bundesbahn
DR	Deutsche Reichbahn
DF	Development Fund
DRF	Depreciation Reserve Fund
DRM	Divisional Railway Manager
ECRS	Economic Contract Responsibilty System
ER	Eastern Railway
ECR	East Central Railway
ECoR	East Coast Railway
EIC	East India Company
EIRC	East India Railway Company

FC	Financial Commissioner
FTRA	Federal Rail Transport Agency
FOC	Freight Operating Company
GIPR	Great India Peninsular Railway
GM	General Manager
GOI	Government of India
GTR	Gross Traffic Receipt
IR	Indian Railways
IRAS	Indian Railway Accounts Service
IRC	Indian Railway Corporation
IRCTC	Indian Railway Catering and Tourism Corporation
IRCON	IRCON International Ltd.
IRFC	Indian Railway Finance Corporation
IRMC	Indian Railway Manufacturing Corporation
IRPS	Indian Railway Personnel Service
JR	Japanese Railways
JNR	Japanese National Railway
JSC	Joint Stock Company
JV	Joint Venture
MOC	Ministry of Communications
MOU	Memorandum of Understanding
NR	Northern Railway
NCR	North Central Railway
NER	North Eastern Railway
NFR	Noth Frontier Railway
NWR	North Western Raiway
NTKM	Net Tonne Kilometer
NTPC	National Thermal Power Corporation
OHE	Over Head Equipmant
OPRAF	Office of Passenger Rail Franchising
OR	Operating Ratio
ORR	Office of Rail Regulator
OWE	Ordinary Working Expenditure
PAT	Profit After Tax
PBT	Profit Before Tax
PESB	Public Enterprises Selection Board
PKM	Passenger Kilometers

PLB	Productivity Linked Bonus
PPP	Public Private Partnership
PSU	Public Sector Undertaking
Rites	Rites Ltd.
RDSO	Research Design and Standards Organisation
ROSCO	Rolling Stock Company
RZhD	Joint Stock Company of Russion Railways
SAIL	Steel Authority of India Ltd.
SR	Sothern Railway
SCR	Soth Central Railway
SCRA	Special Class Railway Apprentice
SER	South Eastern Railway
SECR	South East Central Railway
SJ	Statens Jarnvagar
SSO	Social Service Obligations
SWR	South Western Railway
TKM	Track Kilometer
TKM	Tonne Kilometer
TOC	Train Operating Company
TOPS	Total Operating System
TU	Traffic Unit
TWE	Total Working Expenditure
UBL	Uneconomic Branch Line
UK	United Kingdom
UPSC	Union Public Service Commission
WR	Western Railway
WCR	West Central Railway

Part 1

Introduction

1

Indian Railways

Good, efficient and cheap transport facility is critical for socio-economic development. Whether transport facility on its own can spur growth is a matter of debate, but that its absence impedes growth is universally accepted. Some have even gone to the extent of advocating that transport capacity should be created ahead of demand.

Transport links sources of raw material to centres of production and production centres to consumption centres both within and outside the country. Low transport cost reduces the cost of the product. Of the two main land-based means of transport – roads and railways, the latter has many advantages over road. Railways offer better energy efficiency, least cost and are least polluting. The per unit operating cost of rail is considered to be higher than only one mode of transport, i.e. water. Further, for a given level of traffic the cost of constructing transport facility is said to be six times lower in rail compared to road. Its social cost with respect to damage or destruction to the environment is also significantly lower.

Road, however, scores in terms of lower terminal handling costs, flexibility of operation and door-to-door service. For short distances and for higher value goods, road has been found to be more advantageous. For low traffic volumes also road is preferred to rail.

Nowhere else, other than China, are railways as closely interwoven with the economic and social lives of the people as in India. Indian Railways is considered to be the life-line of the nation. Its importance in India is far different from that in most other countries, particularly United Kingdom, Sweden, France, Germany, Japan, New Zealand etc. All these countries are much smaller. So their rail transport network is also much smaller than that in India. In their case, railways is not the prime source of transport, both in terms of freight as well as passenger transport. Good and efficient alternative means of transport are available. Railways there do not have as much economic, social and strategic role as in India. Their economies are also far stronger and can bear the cost of failure of experiments in rail transport.

> Railways are the only high capacity transport mode that can meet the long term needs of an economy and country of the size of India.[1]

With route length of 64,460 kms Indian Railways is the third largest network after China and Russia. The network extends from Baramulla in the north to Kanyakumari in the south and Dwarka in the west to Ledo in the east. It has 7,133 stations.

In 2011–12, Indian Railways carried 8,224 million passengers and 969.05 million tonnes of freight traffic. Freight traffic during the year 2012–13 was 1012 million tons thereby bringing it into the exclusive club of railways carrying more than a billion tonnes of freight traffic per annum viz. China, Russia and the US railroads. Indian Railways run more than 12,500 passenger trains and 7400 freight trains and on an average carry 23 million passengers and 3 million tonnes of traffic everyday. Indian Railways employs 1.306 million employees and is thus the single biggest employer in the country next to the Indian defence forces.

Indian Railways is a fully government-owned undertaking. It has a separate Minister for Railways who is invariably of the rank of a Cabinet Minister. He is assisted by one or two Minister(s) of State depending upon political compulsions. The Ministry of Railways functions both as a ministry, i.e., the policy-making wing of the government as well as the top executive body, in the form of a Railway Board. Though a government department undertaking, thanks to the Separation Convention of 1924, Indian Railways enjoys a degree of independence both in operational as well as financial matters not generally available to other government departments. It has a separate budget which is separately approved by the Parliament. However, since it is a government-owned undertaking its receipts and expenditure form a part of the general budget of the Government of India.

---

[1] '*Expert Group on Indian Railways, The Indian Railway Report: Policy Imperatives for Reinvention and Growth*', National Council of Applied Economic Research, India 2001, 40.

The Railway Board is headed by a Chairman and six Members viz. the Financial Commissioner, Member Engineering, Member Traffic, Member Mechanical, Member Electrical and Member Staff. The Chairman is ex-officio Principal Secretary and all Members are ex-officio Secretaries in Government of India. Member Traffic looks after both operating and commercial functions of Railways. The Financial Commissioner holds a somewhat special position in the sense that he is also a representative of the Minister of Finance in the Ministry of Railways and in that capacity is expected to keep the Minister of Finance apprised about the affairs of Railways. All Members are assisted by a number of Additional Members and functional Directorates including Directorates for Economics, Planning, Statistics, Health and Security. The Signal and Telecommunications departments are headed by two Additional Members reporting to Member Electrical. The Stores department is headed by an Additional Member reporting to Member Mechanical and Director General Health reporting to Member Staff.

Administratively, the network is divided into 17 zones including Kolkata Metro Rail. Each zone is headed by a General Manager who is assisted by an Additional General Manager and Heads of Departments for each functional department such as Finance, Engineering, Operating, Commercial, Mechanical, Electrical, Signal and Telecommunication, Safety, Stores, Planning, Security and Medical. The General Manager functions within 'negative powers' delegated to him by the Ministry of Railways which means that he has all the powers except for those which are specifically 'not delegated' to him. He reports to the Chairman, Railway Board.

Each zone, except for Kolkata Metro, is further divided into Divisions. There are at present 68 Divisions which are headed by Divisional Railway Managers assisted by one or more Additional Divisional Railway Managers depending on need. The functional structure of a Division is identical to that of a railway zone except that there are no separate departments for Planning and Statistics in the Divisions. These functions are centralised at the level of the zonal headquarter offices. The Stores function is also not 'divisionalised'. Stores depots are located at such places which enables them to serve more than one Division and workshops/repair shops.

Indian Railways is a fully vertically integrated entity in the sense that it undertakes the full gamut of railway operations – from manufacturing its rolling stock, owning, constructing and maintaining its infrastructure, running of trains, carrying out repairs and maintenance of its assets through its workshops and repair shops etc. In fact, Indian Railways is self-sufficient in almost all aspects of its requirements. It is often called a state within state.

Indian Railways has six production units manufacturing locomotives, coaches and wheel sets and a number of repair workshops spread all over the country. Setting up more production units has been announced in the rail budget for 2013–14. These production units and workshops are captive units manufacturing almost entirely for Indian Railways.

In addition, there is a Research Design and Standards Organisation (RDSO), a Central Organisation for Modernisation of Workshops (COFMOW), 16 Public Sector Undertakings and a large number of training institutes for all categories of employees.

Indian Railways has its own network of hospitals and health units providing medical facilities to railway employees and their family members, retired railway employees and their family Members as well as to the civilians of the nearby areas. Facilities also exist to refer railway employees, their family Members and pensioners to other than railway hospitals for specialised treatment.

Indian Railways also runs some schools for the benefit of railway employees. These facilities were created long time back in railway residential colonies where there were either no schools or were of poor standard. It also has a large number of retiring rooms at most of the important stations and run catering services in trains and at stations for the convenience of railway passengers.

Forced by high rates of electricity charged by the state electricity boards/ power supply companies, Indian Railways is now setting up its own power plants for traction purposes.

Capital investment in railways is carried out through three sources – loan from the Government of India, assets acquired through loan from the Indian Railway Finance Corporation (IRFC) and its own internal resources via various Funds viz. Capital Fund, Development Fund (DF), Safety Fund and Depreciation Reserve Fund (DRF). Usually, the loan from the Government of India is also referred to as budgetary support and investment from all other sources, excluding the internal resources, is clubbed as extra budgetary resources. There are well-laid-down rules regarding which type of investment can be financed from which source of fund except in the case of investments to be met through loan from general revenues and investments from Capital Fund. An investment which earlier could be financed only through loan from general revenues can, from 1997, be financed from Capital Fund as well. The actual allocation is decided from project to project. Development Fund is used for financing expenditure on passenger amenities, labour welfare works etc. As the name indicates, the DRF is used for carrying out renewal and replacement nature of work. Although the appropriation to all the internal funds is made from railway revenues through the Budget, one difference needs to be noted. While appropriation to DRF is made from revenue before the calculation of surplus, appropriations to Capital Fund, Development Fund and Safety Fund are made after the calculation of surplus of revenue over expenditure and after payment of Dividend which is the first charge on surplus.

Appropriation to the funds including DRF is not based on any principle. Which means that appropriation to these funds, and hence expenditure from them, is dependent on the financial position of railways during the year. Appropriation to DRF has further significance. Appropriation to DRF (not expenditure from DRF) is part of total expenditure which forms the numerator for the calculation of the Operating Ratio (OR). Hence the amount of appropriation is decided with an eye on its impact on the Operating Ratio. Increase in the appropriation has adverse impact on Operating Ratio and a decrease improves the figures of Operating Ratio. As can be readily seen, this leaves quite a lot of scope for subjectivity. Thus, the OR calculated as at present cannot be said to be an objective index. It is impossible to say what would have been the Operating Ratio of Indian Railways if the appropriation to DRF had been based on some objective principle enabling proper renewal and replacement of assets or on principles of commercial accounting. But this much is well accepted that for the last several years renewals and replacement of assets have suffered badly for want of funds. [For more detailed discussion on the concept of Operating Ratio on Indian Railways please, see my paper titled 'A Modified Operating Ratio'[2]].

Loan from General Revenues, called Capital-at-Charge, is a non-repayable loan on which Indian Railways pays interest called Dividend. The rate of Dividend is decided by the Railway Convention Committee of Parliament every five years keeping in view the average borrowing rate of the government and the financial condition of Railways. Earlier, the rate of Dividend used to be higher than the average borrowing rate of the government. Since the 1980s, it is a little lower. Based on the recommendations of the Railway Convention Committee 2009, the rate of Dividend for the year 2012–13 was 4 per cent.

---

[2] K. B. Verma, 'A Modified Operating Ratio', *Readings in Indian Railway Finance*, ed. K. B. Verma, Academic Foundation, India, 1998.

Some concessions are also available in calculation of Dividend. For example:

- Concessional rate of 3.5 per cent Dividend is applicable on the capital cost of residential buildings.
- Dividend on capital invested on New Lines is deferred during the period of construction and for five years after opening for operation. The Dividend liability is only deferred, not foregone. It has to be paid sixth year onwards from the amount of surplus remaining after the payment of normal Dividend in respect of the new line. However, the unliquidated liability at the end of 20 years from the date of opening gets extinguished.
- Losses on working of strategic lines is borne by General Revenues.
- Losses on 28 national lines taken up after 1.4.1955 on other than financial consideration are borne by the government.

The above list is only indicative, not exhaustive.

Capital investments are normally expected to be financed through loan from the General Revenues. However, since the financial position of the government is itself under stress, the government has not been able to provide as much funds as required by Railways.

Table 1.1: Plan period outlay on Railway (₹ 000 Crs)

	Up to Vth Plan 1950–78	*VIth Plan 1980–85*	*VIIth Plan 1985–90*	*VIIIth Plan 1992–97*	*IXth Plan 1997–2002*	*Xth Plan 2002–07*	*XIth Plan 2007–12*
Total Plan Outlay	60	109	219	486	814	1526	3677
Outlay on Transport	10	14	30	65	118	260	613
Outlay on Railways	5	7	17	32	46	84	191
Transport as % of Total	17	13	14	13	14	17	17
Railway as % of Total	8	6	8	7	6	6	5
Railway as % of Transport Outlay	50	50	56.67	49.23	38.98	32.31	31.16

Note: Rounded Figures. Does not include inter-Plan period 1966–69
Source: Indian Railway Year Book 2011–12

It is seen from Table 1.1 that the while the financial support from the government has been increasing in absolute terms, it has been going down both as a percentage of Total Plan Outlay as well as Outlay on Transport. The percentage of outlay on Railways to Total Plan size has been lowest in the Eleventh Plan.

Table 1.2 shows that except for the First Five Year Plan, quite a substantial part of Railways' investment was met through funds from general revenues. It was highest for a ten-year period from 1970 to 1979–80. It came down to 23 per cent during the Eighth Plan period and is now around 40 per cent or so.

Table 1.2: Financing of Railways' Plans (₹ Crs.)

Plan	*Internal Resources*		*Extra Budgetary Resources*		*Tot Int. & Extra Budget*		*From Gen Rev*		*Total*
	Amt	*% age*	*Amt*	*% age*	*Amt*	*% age*	*Amt*	*% age*	*Outlay*
I	280	66	...	...	280	66	142	34	422
II	467	45	...	...	467	45	576	55	1043
III	545	32	...	...	545	32	1140	68	1685
1966–69	320	42	...	...	320	42	442	58	762
IV	397	28	...	...	397	28	1031	72	1428
V	384	25	...	...	384	25	1141	75	1525
1978–80	316	25	...	...	316	25	935	75	1251
VI	2783	42	...	...	2783	42	3802	58	6585
VII	7089	43	2520	15	9609	58	6940	42	16549
1990–91	2091	43	1092	23	3183	66	1632	34	4815
1991–92	2134	40	1503	28	3637	67	1756	33	5393
VIII	18832	58	6161	19	24993	77	7313	23	32306
IX	15737	35	14003	31	29740	66	15411	34	45151
X	25871	33	16981	21	42852	54	36362	46	79214
XI	66317	36	46978	25	113295	61	72989	39	186284

Source: Compiled by author

Lack of adequate funds from the government for investment has had two effects on railway investments.

- It has forced Railways to increasingly depend on internal resources for investment. And since Railway finances are already stressed, it has resulted into paucity of funds for investment. So much so that in 2011–12 no funds could be spared for Appropriation to as critical a fund as the Safety Fund.

The increasing dependence on internal finances is reflected in the falling ratio of Capital-at-Charge with respect to Total Investment as shown in Table 1.3. There has been some upturn from 2009–10. Depending on internal resources may not be bad in itself, provided the situation of internal resources so permits.

- The second impact has been that it has forced Railways to look to external capital through IRFC which is at a much higher rate of interest, further straining the financial position of railways.

Table 1.3: Capital-at-Charge vis-a-vis Total Investment (₹ Crs.)

Year	*Cap-at Charge*	*Total Investment*	*% Cap to Total Invest.*
1950–51	827	855.2	96.70
1960–61	1520.9	1868.6	81.39
1970–71	3330.3	4099.4	81.24
1980–81	6096.3	7448.4	81.85
1990–91	16125.8	22200.5	72.64
2000–01	43051.88	63341.01	67.97
2003–04	56061.79	87474.5	64.09
2004–05	59346.93	98490.02	60.26
2005–06	65878.37	112180.41	58.73
2006–07	76030.69	130168.71	58.41
2007–08	88521.14	151434.35	58.46
2008–09	104301.25	176726.41	59.02
2009–10	123000.69	203305.37	60.50
2010–11	143220.57	231615.25	61.84
2011–12	161447.97	257958.35	62.59

Source: Compiled by author

The capital raised by IRFC from the market was originally intended to be used only for financing procurement of rolling stock for railways. It is now used for other purposes also, but in a limited way. Up to 2011–12. IRFC had financed rolling stock procurement by Railways to the tune of ₹ 82,447 Crs. Rolling stock procured through IRFC are on lease to Railways for which Railways pay leasing charges (now known as hire purchase) consisting of three elements – interest paid by IRFC on the borrowing from the market, amortisation charges and a nominal commission. At the end of the lease period the asset becomes the property of Railways.

However, as against the attractive prospect of paying off the debt as in the case of loan from IRFC, it has been held that a loan in perpetuity as currently structured is, perhaps, not all that bad.

> The expert study in question was undertaken by Jawaharlal Nehru University at the instance of the Railway Capital Restructuring Committee (RCRC 1995). It concluded that even allowing for the obligation to pay Dividend in perpetuity on capital provided by the government, this funding option was definitely cheaper than the leasing arrangement through IRFC.[3]

Table 1.4: Internal resources and market borrowing (₹ Crs)

Plan	*Internal Resources*	*Borrowings*	*Total*	*% Internal to Total*	*% Borrow to Total*
I	280	...	280	100	...
II	467	...	467	100	...
III	545	...	545	100	...
1966–69	320	...	320	100	...
IV	397	...	397	100	...
V	384	...	384	100	...
1978–80	316	...	316	100	...
VI	2783	...	2783	100	...
VII	7089	2520	9609	74	26
1990–91	2091	1092	3183	66	34
1991–92	2134	1503	3637	59	41
VIII	18832	6161	24993	75	25
IX	15737	14003	29740	53	47
X	25871	16981	42852	60	40
XI	66317	46978	113295	59	41

Source: Compiled by author

While this may be true at the present rate of Dividend it may not remain so at higher rates of Dividend. A small exercise in the Annexure shows that the cut-off point is reached at around 8.5 per cent. This is relevant in view of consistent demand by the Ministry of Finance to increase the Dividend to 9 per cent.

---

[3] Ibid.

Borrowings from the market has increased the burden of cost of capital on Railways. In the context of Indian Railways the cost of capital may be looked at from two angles: one in which the cost of capital is related to the amount of debt such as Dividend on Capital-at-Charge or interest paid on IRFC loans. While this is quite understandable, cost of capital needs to be related also to capacity to pay of Railways. In Table 1.5, Dividend and payment of interest (not Total Lease Charges) to IRFC are clubbed as the cost of capital.

Thus, if Dividend is related to Capital-at-Charge the ratio works out to 3.5 per cent to 4 per cent. It works out to an average of 9 per cent of Ordinary Working Expenses and 6 per cent of Gross Traffic Receipts. And the ratio shoots up to 14.6 per cent if the payment of Dividend plus interest paid to IRFC is related to Ordinary Working Expenses and to 9.75 if related to Gross Traffic Earnings.

Table 1.5: Burden of cost of capital (₹ Crs)

Year	*OWE*	*GTR*	*Dividend*	*Interest to IRFC*	*Total Payment*	*% Div to OWE*	*% Div to GTR*	*% Total to OWE*	*% Total to GTR*
2000–01	26446	34880	2131	1660	3791	8.06	6.11	14.33	10.87
2001–02	27581	37838	2337	1820	4157	8.47	6.18	15.07	10.99
2002–03	28401	41068	2665	1736	4401	9.38	6.49	15.50	10.72
2003–04	29305	42905	3087	1688	4775	10.53	7.19	16.29	11.13
2004–05	31711	47370	2716	1662	4378	8.56	5.73	13.81	9.24
2005–06	33414	54491	3005	1699	4704	8.99	5.51	14.08	8.63
2006–07	35713	62732	3584	1875	5459	10.04	5.71	15.29	8.70
2007–08	39356	71720	4239	2153	6392	10.77	5.91	16.24	8.91
2008–09	52535	79862	4718	2910	7628	8.98	5.91	14.52	9.55
2009–10	63551	86964	5543	3115	8658	8.72	6.37	13.62	9.96
2010–11	65346	94356	4941	3503	8444	7.56	5.24	12.92	8.95
2011–12	71083	104110	5656	4142	9798	7.96	5.43	13.78	9.41
Average						9.00	5.98	14.62	9.75

Note: OWE is Ordinary Working Expenses and GTR is Gross Traffic Receipts
Source: Compiled by author

The earnings of Indian Railways arise from three sources – freight traffic, passenger traffic and miscellaneous earnings consisting mainly of earnings from parcel traffic, Dividend from railway PSUs such as IRCON, Rites etc. and fees collected by Railway Service Commissions. In 2011–12, freight earnings accounted for more than 67 per cent of the earnings, passenger about 27 per cent and miscellaneous earnings for the balance 6 per cent or so (Table 1.6).

There are only ten commodities which account for 93 per cent and only four commodities that account for about 70 per cent of freight earnings. It will be seen that carrying coal is the life blood of Indian Railways so much so that the gap between earnings from coal and the second highest earning commodity iron ore is stupendous. Of these ten commodities, all are low rated except for two viz. Exim containers and the Domestic containers which can be called somewhat higher rated but which taken together account for only about 5 per cent of the earnings. This is partly because of the nature of freight transport itself. Due to various reasons, high rated consignments generally move by road. In the case of Indian Railways this has been further reinforced by unduly high freight rates in recent years.

Table 1.6: Structure of freight traffic 2011–12

Commodity	*₹ (Crs)*	*Percentage of Total*
Coal	28,178.96	41.6
Iron ore	7411.13	10.94
Cement	6409.83	9.46
Foodgrains	4911.92	7.25
Iron and Steel	3925.81	5.8
Fertilizers	3772.45	5.57
Mineral Oils	3623.64	5.35
Exim Containers	2480.09	3.66
Limestone	1319.64	1.95
Domestic Containers	888.97	1.31
Total Ten Commodities	62,922.44	92.89
Total All Commodities	69,547.59	100

Source: Indian Railway Year Book 2011–12

Position in respect of passenger traffic is shown in Table 1.7 . The skewed relationship between the volume of passenger traffic of different types and earnings from them is too glaring to be commented upon. In Indian Railways passenger fares have always been kept somewhat depressed. Freight subsidises passenger traffic and upper class passenger traffic subsidises lower class passenger traffic. Actually, cross-subsidisation of traffic, particularly of passenger traffic, is not a phenomenon unique to Indian Railways.

Table 1.7: Structure of passenger traffic 2011–12

Type	*Nos. (Mil)*	*Percentage*	*Rev ₹ (Cr)*	*Percentage*
Non-Sub				
Upper Class	112	1.36	7,851.69	27.8
Second Class (Mail/Exp)	1,188	14.45	14,560.31	51.54
Second Class Ordy	2547	30.96	3,908.78	13.84
Total Non-Suburban	3847	46.78	26,320.78	93.18
Suburban	4377	53.22	1,925.65	6.82
Total	12071	100	28,246.43	100

Source: Indian Railway Year Book 2011–12

Except for a marginal increase of fares in the Budget for 2013–14, passenger fares have remained untouched for more than a decade due to political reasons, forcing railways to increase freight rates to unreasonably high levels driving freight traffic away from railways. This has led to skewed relationship between per PKM earnings and per NTKM earnings. Recently in June, 2014 passenger fare has been increased by 14.2% and freight rates by 6.5%. In addition some fine tuning in railway tariffs is also permitted by linking tariff adjustment in response to increase in fuel charges. Table 1.8 represents traffic unit cost and unit revenue.

Table 1.8: Traffic unit cost and unit revenue (in Paise)

Year	*Coaching Services*			*Freight Services*			*Ratios*	
	Cost Per PKM	*Earnings Per PKM*	*Ratio %age*	*Cost Per NTKM*	*Earnings Per NTKm*	*Ratio % age*	*Cost PKM/ NTKM*	*Earnings PKM/ NTKM*
2000–01	38.03	22.97	60.4	60.56	74.61	123.2	62.80	30.79
2001–02	37.98	22.66	59.7	58.44	74.56	127.6	64.99	30.39
2002–03	38.74	24.38	62.9	57.01	75.04	131.6	67.95	32.49
2003–04	40.59	24.53	60.4	50.89	72.44	142.3	79.76	33.86
2004–05	40.31	24.52	60.8	54.76	75.55	138.0	73.61	32.46
2005–06	39.40	24.53	62.3	54.35	82.55	151.9	72.49	29.72
2006–07	39.41	24.75	62.8	51.8	86.73	167.4	76.08	28.54
2007–08	39.96	25.74	64.4	52.14	90.98	174.5	76.64	28.29
2008–09	48.86	26.13	53.5	63.74	96.9	152.0	76.66	26.97
2009–10	52.87	25.96	49.1	65.84	97.41	147.9	80.30	26.65

Source: Compiled by author

As far as coaching services are concerned, the cost recovery (i.e., the ratio of earnings per PKM to costs per PKM) has been only around 50 per cent or so during the last decade while it is around 150 per cent in respect of freight services. And while the ratio of PKM/NTKM cost was 80 per cent in 2009–10 the ratio in respect of earnings was only 27 per cent which is one of the lowest in the world. The increase in per unit earnings also has not kept pace with increase in costs.

The imbalance in increases in costs and earnings over a period of time is also seen from Table 1.9. The index of increase in per unit cost of coaching traffic is 139 while the index of increase in earnings is only 113. On the other hand the index of increase in per unit cost of freight traffic is 109 while the index of increase in earnings is 131. This again highlights the lop-sided structure of fares and freights.

Table 1.9: Growth of traffic costs and earnings (in ₹)

Year	*Cost Per PKM*	*Index*	*Earnings Per PKM*	*Index*	*Cost Per NTKM*	*Index*	*Earnings Per NTKM*	*Index*
2000–01	38.03	100	22.97	100	60.56	100	74.61	100
2001–02	37.98	100	22.66	99	58.44	96	74.56	100
2002–03	38.74	102	24.38	106	57.01	94	75.04	101
2003–04	40.59	107	24.53	107	50.89	84	72.44	97
2004–05	40.31	106	24.52	107	54.76	90	75.55	101
2005–06	39.40	104	24.53	107	54.35	90	82.55	111
2006–07	39.41	104	24.75	108	51.8	86	86.73	116
2007–08	39.96	105	25.74	112	52.14	86	90.98	122
2008–09	48.86	128	26.13	114	63.74	105	96.90	130
2009–10	52.87	139	25.96	113	65.84	109	97.41	131

Source: Compiled by author

The Railway Budget is required to be approved by the Parliament. But it is only the expenditure part of the Budget, both operating expenditure and capital expenditure, which requires the approval of the Parliament. Not the revenue part. Thus means that fares and freights do not require the approval of Parliament. But that is not to say that there is no political influence on fixing of fares and freights. They still require the approval of the Railway Minister where political rather than financial considerations play more important part.

Conventionally, increases in fares and freights are indicated in the Railway Budget. But mid-year revisions are also not unknown.

Besides fares and freights, railway investments too are worst affected by political influence. But it would be unfair to say that this is something quite peculiar to Indian Railways. Government-owned railways all over the world have been subject to strong political influence in all matters, most of all in respect of investment decisions.

Investment decisions in Indian Railways are very highly centralised. Projects costing up to ₹ 300 Crs. are required to be approved only by the Minister for Railways before incorporation in the Railway Budget. However, projects relating to new lines, gauge conversion, railway electrification and metropolitan railway projects, are required to be appraised by the Planning Commission before being put up for approval of the Minister for Railways. Projects above ₹ 300 Crs. are first submitted to the Planning Commission for its 'in-principle' approval. They are then submitted to the Expanded Board for Railways (EBR) for clearance. EBR consists of representatives of Ministry of Finance, Ministry of Statistics and Program Implementation and the Planning Commission. A Cabinet note is then prepared for inter-ministerial consultation with the concerned ministries including the Ministry of Finance. They are then put up to the Cabinet Committee on Investments (CCI). After the clearance of the CCI the projects are included in the Railway Budget for approval of the Parliament.

The figures from the Railway Budget 2011–12 in Table 1.10 give some idea of finances of Indian Railways.

Table 1.10: Financial results 2011–12

Decsription	*(Amt in ₹ Crs)*
Capital-at-charge	122,772.04
Inv. From Capital Fund	38,675.93
Total Investment*	161,447.97
Passenger Earnings	28,246.43
Goods Earnings	69,547.59
Misc. Earnings**	6,359.53
Gross Earnings	**104,110.36**
Ordy. Working Expenses	74,537.41
App. To DRF	6,520.00

Contd.

Contd.

Decsription	*(Amt in ₹ Crs)*
App. To Pension Fund	17,610.00
Total Working Expenses	98,667.41
Total Traffic Receipts	**5,442.95**
Misc. Transactions	1,338.66
Net Revenue	**6,781.60**
Dividend	5,656.03
Surplus	**1,125.57**
App. To Capital Fund	
App to Developt Fund	
App to Safety Fund	
Operating Ratio	94.85
% of Net Revenue to Capital	4.2

Note: * Does not include investments from DRF, DF and Safety Fund.
**Miscellaneous Earnings shown above is not strictly according to the classification in Railway Budget. It includes earnings classified as 'Sundries' which is not a part of Gross Earnings. It has been done here for the sake of simplicity.
Source: Compiled by author

Indian Railways calculate OR which is defined as the ratio of Total Expenditure to Gross Earnings. It will be seen that the OR of about 95 leaves very little for payment of Dividend and apportionment to Funds. OR is calculated for Indian Railways as a whole as well as for each individual zonal railway. But OR is not calculated for the Divisions.

For quite some time, the finances of Indian Railways have been in acute distress which has adversely affected every aspect of railway working. Safety records have drawn a lot of flak. The quality of service has been deteriorating. It has been consistently losing traffic to road. Projects are unduly delayed. Railway finances have been in such poor shape that in many years Indian Railways had to defer payment of full Dividend to the General Revenues. The deferred Dividend liability could be cleared only in 2007–08. However, even in the worst years, unlike many other undertakings of the Government of India and almost all government-owned railways of the world, Indian Railways has been consistently able to generate operating profits. The financial performance of Indian Railways is given in further detail in Chapter 3.

2

Historical Background

Like almost all railways of the world, Indian Railways owes its origin to private initiative. The earliest idea of a railway system in India was conceived by a group of merchants in Manchester, England in the 1830s. They looked upon India as a source of cheap raw material, particularly cotton, as well as a huge market for British manufactured goods, mainly cotton textile. But not much came out of it until the incorporation of East India Railway Company (EIRC) in 1845 as a joint stock company. About 90 per cent of the capital of the company was owned by British interest and the entire capital of the company was in the form of equity rather than debt. But the private investors were hesitant in investing in a railway system in a land which was too distant, largely unknown to them and politically uncertain. As it so happened, the East India Company (EIC) was also keen for a railway system in India as it saw in it great commercial and military advantage. But EIC did not have the financial wherewithal to undertake such a venture on its own. Therefore, it encouraged the railway company to finance, construct and manage a railway system in India. Many rounds of negotiation followed culminating into signing an Agreement on 18 April 1849.

The main terms of the Agreement were:

- East India Company (henceforth called 'the Company') would select the route, gauge and direction of the line to be constructed.
- The Company would provide land free of cost for the lines, station buildings, offices and other facilities.
- Fares and freights would be approved by the Company.
- The Company would guarantee a return of 5 per cent per annum on the capital invested by East India Railway Company (henceforth called 'the Railway Company') for a period of 25 years.

- In case of a shortfall in any year, the Company would make up for the balance.
- If in any year, the return was more than 5 per cent, half of the excess over 5 per cent would be paid to the Company to compensate for payments made by the Company in earlier years. Half the balance may be retained by the railway company. This arrangement would continue till the compensatory payments by East India Company were wiped out.
- The rate of exchange for remittance of the guaranteed money was fixed at 22 shillings per Rupee.
- All expenses of the railway company would be subject to sanction of the EIC.
- All earnings of the railway company will be first deposited into the coffers of the EIC.
- Railways will become the property of the Company after 99 years against payment for all assets as per valuation at that time.
- Although the railway company could sell the railway to the EIC at any time before 99 years, the EIC could purchase the Railways only within 6 months of the expiration of 25 years and 50 years on conditions agreeable to both parties.
- The staff of the railway company, its accounts and affairs would be subject to the control of the EIC.

Three elements of the above Agreement are worth noting. One is that the EIC committed to provide land free of cost. This reduced the capital expenditure of the railway company substantially. Second was the guaranteed return on investment. Thirdly, although the entire investment was being made by a private company, the EIC had considerable control on the railway company.

The above arrangement is famously known as the Guarantee System as it guaranteed to the investors a particular return on investment as well as a fixed rate of exchange between Rupee and Pound Sterling. Thus, the interest of the investors was fully protected.

Another important railway company, the Great Indian Peninsula Railway (GIPR) based on similar conditions was incorporated in 1949. While the EIRC had its area of operation in the east, GIPR had its domain in the western part of the country. Though incorporated later, GIPR was first off the mark. The first train ran between Bori Bunder (Mumbai) and Thane for a distance of 33 kms on 16 August 1853 that is within a period of four years of inception of GIPR.

Similar agreements were entered into by the Government of India in England (the interests of the Company were taken over by the British Crown in 1857) with other railway companies in 1860s and 1870s with slightly varying conditions and guarantees varying from 4.5 per cent to 5 per cent depending upon market rate of interest at the time. The Government in Delhi was in no way involved in the negotiations leading to some dissatisfaction in the Government at Delhi.

Two points need to be noted over here. First, this was perhaps the earliest example of Public Private Partnership (PPP) in India. Secondly, the guaranteed return was in relation to investment and had nothing to do with earnings or profit of the company. And it is on this latter account that the Guarantee System has often been criticised. It is argued that since a return on capital expenditure was guaranteed, there was no incentive for the railway companies to economise. On the contrary, extravagance was more rewarding. The Guarantee System understandably led to extravagance not only in capital expenditure but in working expenses as well, laying the seeds of unforeseen liability on the finances of the Government of India.

While this may be true, it is doubtful whether railway development in India would have at all taken place without the Guarantee System. It did encourage private investment in Railways in India. So much so that by 1868, Pound Sterling 70 million worth of investment was made in railways in India.

However, the Guarantee System led to great strain on the Budget of the Government of India. The construction costs turned out to be much more than estimated – 20,000 pounds per mile against initial estimate of 12,000 pounds which was much higher than 16,000 pounds per mile for similar construction in Australia. Further, while the guaranteed interest had to be paid by the government to the railway companies right from the commencement of investment, there was as natural in most infrastructure projects no earnings during construction and for some years after construction as well. In fact the earnings were never very good. The guaranteed rate of exchange also worked to the disadvantage of the government. The actual rate of exchange turned out to be not more than 20 shillings as against guaranteed 22 shillings. All these factors lead to heavy strain on government finances.

After 1880, the Government of India started acquiring many of the guaranteed Railways and financing railway construction itself. The railways so financed by the Government of India were, however, mostly constructed and managed by private companies through construction and management contracts. The acquisition of the railways had another adverse impact on Government of India budget. The Government of India became directly responsible for working expenditure of the railways.

This had some very adverse results:

- Since railway revenues accounted for more than half of Government of India (GOI) revenues, any swing in railway revenues resulted in consequent swings in GOI budget. This was a common annual phenomenon as railway revenues were very much affected by uncertainty in harvest which in turn was dependent upon the vagaries of the monsoon.
- In the years when GOI revenues were strained, capital works in railways were the first casualty.
- Due to uncertainty in revenues of the government, many a times funds for railway works were allocated as late as February or even March to be spent by the end of March.
- Apart from the dismal financial scenario, there was dissatisfaction amongst the Indian population on account of very little role of local talent in the management of railways.

Therefore, when the management contract with East India Railway Company became due for renewal, the British Government appointed a committee in 1920 under the Chairmanship of Sir William Mitchell Acworth (1850–1925), famously known as the Acworth Committee to go into the affairs of railways in India. The Committee submitted its report in 1921.

No committee on Indian Railways before or after independence has had such momentous impact on the character of railway business and government railway relationship in India as the Acworth Committee. It changed the entire philosophy of the railways financial management in India.

Some of the observations of the Committee appear to be equally applicable today and are reproduced below verbatim.

> 28. 'The defects mentioned in the last Chapter are primarily due to the failure of the Government to provide the Railways with adequate funds for capital expenditure on development and extension, and even for essential operations of renewal and repairs. They are the inevitable result of a paralysing system which has not been adapted and developed to meet the requirements of what is essentially a commercial enterprise of the first magnitude.'

58 '.... We do not think that the Indian Railways can be modernised, improved and enlarged, so as to give India the service of which it is in crying need at the moment, nor that the Railways can yield to the Indian public the financial return which they are entitled to expect from so valuable a property until the whole financial methods are radically reformed. And the essence of reform is contained in two things: (1) the complete separation of the railway budget from the general budget of the country; and its reconstruction in a form which frees a great commercial business from the trammels of a system which assumes that a concern goes out of business on each 31st of March and recommences de novo on the 1st of April; and (2) the emancipation of the railway management from the control of the Finance Department. The primary function of any such Department is to reduce to a minimum expenditure in order to keep to a minimum the corresponding taxation. Its officials are not qualified either by training or experience to judge the essentially commercial and technical question where and when the circumstances of a railway undertaking justify bold undertaking of large sums, having regard not merely to the actual condition of the physical machine at the moment, but to the prospects of development and the requirement of the future.'

59 .... It confuses two different things: the functions of Government as government. and the functions of Government as the owner of a great commercial undertaking.,,,,,, It is merely a question of allowing the railway undertaking to finance its own requirements out of its own resources and at its own time.

62 ... We cannot but feel that the authorities responsible for Indian Railway finance ... have entirely failed to appreciate the position of the Indian Railways as a commercial undertaking.

Para 74 '...... we wish to disclaim any idea that the railway organisation should be independent, an imperium in imperio. This is quite out of the question. The Indian Government owns the Railways; the Indian government control them. But that is no reason why the control should take the form which is found suitable in respect of other departments of the State.... the Railways should have a separate budget of their own and assume the responsibilities for earning and expending their own income. The first charge on that income, after paying working expenses, is interest on debt incurred by state for railway purposes ...... whether the railway should pay precisely this amount, or a larger amount, in consideration of the fact that in early years taxation had to be imposed to meet that portion of interest which railway receipts did not cover, or a smaller amount, in consideration of the expenditure which the Railways have since

> incurred for non-railway purposes, is a matter of argument. We have no wish to express a positive opinion, though we think that there is much to be said for letting bygones be bygones and fixing the payment to the Government at the same sum that the Government has itself to find at the present time for interest on railway debt. The point is that the Railway Department, subject to the general control of the Government once it has met its liability to its creditors, should itself regulate the disposal of the balance, and should be free to devote it to new capital purpose (whether directly or as security for new debt incurred) or to reserves or to dissipate it in the form either of reduction of rates or improvement of services.

The main points of the Committee's recommendation can be summarised as follows:

- Railway Budget should be separated from the general budget of the Government of India in order to lend some certainty to government revenues and also to enable railways to manage their finances themselves.
- The Committee repeatedly emphasised that railways is a commercial enterprise and should be treated as such.
- Railways should be allowed freedom to manage their investments and finances according to commercial considerations.
- The role of government should be that of an owner of a commercial enterprise, i.e., a shareholder.
- Since the government owns the railways, it must exercise control on Railways but not in the same manner as it does in the case of other departments of the government.
- Railways must pay an interest to the government at the same rate as the government pays on the loans taken by it to finance its investment in railways.

During the last ninety years the only recommendation which can be said to have been implemented is the separation of railway budget from the general budget of the Government of India.

The recommendations of the Acworth Committee were considered by the Legislative Assembly of the Government of India in 1924 which recommended to the Legislative Council that:

- In order to relieve general budget from the violent fluctuations caused by the incorporation therein of the railway estimates and to enable railways to carry out a continuous railway policy based on the necessity of making a definite return to general revenue on the money expended by the State on Railways.

The railway finances shall be separated from general finances of the country and the general revenues shall receive a definite annual contribution from railways which shall be the first charge on the net receipts of railways.

- The contribution shall be based on the capital-at-charge and working results of commercial lines, and shall be a sum equal to one per cent on the capital-at-charge of commercial lines (excluding capital contributed by companies and Indian States) – plus one fifth of any surplus profits remaining after payment of this fixed return, subject to the condition that, if in any year railway revenues are insufficient to provide the percentage of one per cent on the capital-at-charge, surplus profits in next or subsequent years will not deemed to have accrued for purposes of division until such deficiency has been made good.
- The interest on capital-at-charge of, and the loss in working strategic lines shall be borne by general revenue and shall consequently be deducted from the contribution so calculated in order to arrive at the net amount payable from railway to general revenue each year.
- Any surplus remaining after this payment to general revenue shall be transferred to a railway reserve; provided that if the amount available for transfer to the railway reserve exceeds in any year three crores of rupees, only two-thirds of the excess over three crores shall be transferred to the railway reserve and the remaining one-third shall accrue to general revenue.
- The railway reserve shall be used to secure the payment of the annual contribution to general revenues; to provide, if necessary, for arrears of depreciation and for writing down and writing of capital; and to strengthen the financial position of railways in order that the services rendered to the public may be improved and rates may be reduced.

6. A Standing Finance Committee for railways shall be constituted consisting of Members of the Legislative Assembly.
7. The Railway Department shall place the estimate of railway expenditure before the Standing Finance Committee before discussion of demand for grants for railways.

8. The railway budget shall be presented in advance of the general budget and separate days shall be allotted for its discussion.
9. The railway services should be rapidly Indianised, and further that Indians should be appointed as Members of the Railway Board as early as possible.

The above recommendations are known as the Separation Convention and were accepted in 1924. It may be noted that while the Acworth Committee recommended an interest from railways at the same rate as the government has to pay for loans raised by it for railway investments, the Legislative Assembly did not establish any such relationship. It recommended an interest of 1 per cent only plus a share of profit. Thus, the principle of dual return – a fixed return and a variable return was enunciated, which could be of use even today.

Payment of a small fixed return plus a share of profit was a very sensible option. The then Government of India acted like a cautious shareholder. It refrained from burdening the railways too much as it saw many other advantages of a railway system. At the same time, like any other owner of a commercial venture, wanted a share in its prosperity. This model could very well be adopted for Indian Railways today.

The above measures made fundamental departure from the established system. The government of the day must be complimented for their foresight and courage in accepting such drastic recommendations. The basic principles which it set up have withstood the test time for almost a century and have remained more or less the same till today.

Some important principles which were enunciated are of interest to us –

- Railways to pay a pre-determined rate of interest on capital invested by the Government of India plus a share of profit.
- Interest was to be paid only on the debt raised by the government specifically for investment in railways, and
- The interest was not to be paid on the entire capital. Some concessions were allowed – a principle which is still being followed.
- On certain types of investments, losses in working expenses were allowed to be deducted from the payments due to general revenues.

It needs to be noted that repayment of loan by railways to the general revenues was not contemplated. Thus, in effect, the loan became a loan in perpetuity.

Apart from revision of rates of Dividend from time to time, some important changes in principles were made by different Railway Convention Committees subsequently after independence. Some of the important changes are summarised below.

The Convention Committee of 1949 recommended that:

- The rate of Dividend would include an element of contribution from railways to the general revenues over and above the bare interest paid by the government on the capital provided for railways.
- The annual Dividend shall be 4 per cent of the capital invested and at the end of five years a Committee of the House would review the rate of Dividend having regard to the financial position of Railways and the Average Borrowing Rate of the government and any other relevant factor.
- A Development Fund be constituted for financing expenditure on
  - (i) Passenger amenities
  - (ii) Labour welfare, and
  - (iii) Railway projects which are necessary but not remunerative.

The above recommendations form the fundamental principles for deciding the rate of Dividend even today.

It needs to be noted that besides raising the rate of Dividend, the Convention Committee of 1949 linked the rate of Dividend to the Average Borrowing Rate of the government as against the earlier provision according to which the rate of Dividend was linked to the actual interest paid by the government for loan raised by it specifically for financing investment in railways. Till mid-seventies or so, the Average Borrowing Rate was lower than the rate of Dividend. After that it has been higher. Perhaps because the present state of railway finances may not be able to bear the Average Borrowing Rate of the Government. This swing of the pendulum – sometimes in favour of railways and sometimes in favour of the government is not good.

Later in this book it has been suggested that the entire capital-at-charge at present should be converted into equity by the government. In that case Dividend will become a share of profit rather than an interest on loan. If that does not happen, it needs to be considered whether the original structure of two-part return (Separation Convention 1924), a small fixed return plus a variable return, should not be restored.

The next Convention Committee to make important change of principle was the Committee of 1965. The Committee proposed splitting up the capital-at-charge of Railways into two parts – each having separate rates of Dividend. It recommended that the rate of Dividend on capital up to 1963–64 should be at 5.5 per cent and that on additional capital added from 1 April 1964 it should be paid at 6 per cent. It, thus, enunciated a principle of differential rate of Dividend, slightly different from the earlier two-part return. This, however, was not accepted by the Parliament.

The Convention Committee of 1980 also recommended differential rates of Dividend to which the Ministry of Finance had also agreed. It recommended a rate of 6 per cent on capital invested up to 31 March 1980 (inclusive of 1.5 per cent on capital invested up to 31 March 1964 for payment to States in lieu of Passenger Fare Tax etc.) and 6.5 per cent on capital invested thereafter.

The next important development was setting up of Capital Fund with effect from 1 April 1992 as a result of the recommendation of the Convention Committee of 1991. This Fund was created to finance part of the capital expenditure. After appropriation to Development Fund, the 'Excess' is appropriated to Capital Fund. Thus, like the Depreciation Reserve Fund, Pension Fund and the Development Fund, the Capital Fund also is financed purely from internal resources of Railways.

The Convention Committee of 1998, however, gave up the principle of differentiated rate of Dividend and recommended that the Dividend on the entire capital be paid at 7 per cent irrespective of the year of investment.

The Committee of 1998 made an important observation regarding the cost of social burdens being borne by railways.

> Considering the budgetary support from General Exchequer being reduced from the level of 75% in the Fifth Plan to 23% in the Eighth Plan and the increasing dependence of the Railways on market borrowings, the Committee feel that any unilateral increase in the rate of Dividend without compensating the Indian Railways for carrying social obligations will only put additional pressure on the already strained Railway finances. ….. In this connection, the Committee wish to point out that on the basis of the recommendations made by the Railway Convention Committee (1991) in their Twelfth Report, an Inter-Ministerial Working Group consisting of representatives of Ministry of Railways, Ministry of Finance and Planning Commission was constituted to look into the social obligations borne by the Railways. The Working Group had submitted its unanimous Report in May, 1997 wherein the Social

Service Obligation borne by Railways in 1994–95 was reassessed at ₹ 886 cr. The Committee are constrained to note with disapproval the attitude of the Ministry of Finance of not agreeing to the unanimous recommendation of the Working Group for compensating the Railways on this reduced scale. The Committee recommend that the unanimous recommendation of the Working Group to which the Ministry of Finance was also a party should be accepted without any further delay.

The Committee recommend that

> In order to give the Indian Railways a level playing field with other modes of transportation, the Indian Railways need to be compensated under various heads like losses incurred on transportation of essential commodities, subsidised movement to North Eastern States, operation of unremunerative lines, commuter services etc. The above losses should become explicit charges on the allocations made to the various Central Ministries of the Government to cover specific areas of social responsibility thereby relieving Railways of this burden in order to operate as a commercial enterprise.[1]

The above recommendation has not yet been accepted.

Subsequent Convention Committees did not make any change of principle. They continued with the principle of 1949 and basically confined themselves to changes in the rate of Dividend.

---

[1] *Railway Convention Committee Report*, 1998.

3

Why Reform?

The Rationale for reform

Usually, there are two reasons for reform. One, when a system is not able to perform the way it was designed to perform. Or when the external environment of the system has so metamorphosed, expectations have so changed that the design itself has become obsolete. In respect of organisational structures, it is usually a combination of both. Sometimes charismatic leaders also emerge who are able to see opportunities that others are not able to see.

Where does Indian Railways stand? Are reforms necessary because Indian Railways has failed to deliver or because the external environment has changed, or because expectations from it have changed? Or all three?

The second and third reasons are quite obvious and easy to concede. There has been complete metamorphosis of the transport market due to the growth of other modes of transport. And the potentiality of Indian Railways to play a critical role in the development of the country is also undisputed. Both these aspects have been discussed in Chapter 1 on 'Indian Railways'.

The first one, i.e., whether Indian Railways has failed to deliver, is not so clear. It is rather a mixed bag. But this leads to some further questions. How does one find out whether Indian Railways has failed to deliver? Can there be any objective yardstick? Can failure to meet expectations be construed as failure to perform? Considering the limitation of design, could the expectations themselves not be unrealistic? There are no straight answers. The answers would depend on – the level of inputs, labour practices, external influences, government policies and priorities and so on.

One way to judge performance is by comparison with established norms. As obvious no norms exist or are possible in case of railway industry. Where no norms exist or are possible, the next best alternatives are inter-firm and inter-period comparisons. But inter-firm comparisons are meaningful only in the case of homogeneous entities, not between heterogeneous entities though they may belong to the same genre or nature of business. For example, Indian Railways and German Railways are in rail transport industry. However, they cannot be said to be homogenous entities and are, therefore, not strictly comparable. On the other hand, inter-period comparison suffers from the danger that it can continue to camouflage or paper-over hidden inefficiencies, particularly those of systemic kind. Thus, both types of comparisons suffer from their own limitations. However, inter-period comparison is lesser of the two evils. While inter-firm comparison between dissimilar entities is totally invalid, inter-period comparison is at least able to show whether the entity is improving or not, though it would fail to show whether the performance could have been better.

Productivity of Indian Railways and others

Still, it is worthwhile taking a look at some basic statistics about some major railways of the world vis-à-vis Indian Railways (Table 3.1).

Table 3.1: Productivity of Indian Railways and others

	Unit	*India*	*China*	*Russia*	*France*	*Germany*	*S. Africa*
Route	Kms	63465	62200	85245	29286	34218	20247
Locos	Nos	7910	16453	12213	4588	4787	2646
Coaches	Nos	37119	40328	....	15879	20305	3251
Wagons	Nos	22379	541824	...	35456	1567	94210
Passenger	Mill Nos	53780	1106512	133871	96274	178546	3102
PKM	Mill	575702	583320	172217	76159	92554	991
Freight	Mill Tons	602	2309	1281	130	275	182
NTKM	Mill	507398	1934612	1858100	41898	88022	109721
Staff	000s	1422	1666	1162	167	225	33

Source: India: Railway Sector Improvement Program, ADB Technical Assistance Consultant's Report, Project No. 36330-02.

Route km-wise there are only three railways which are comparable (except for USA), viz. Russia, India and China. Output-wise China (25,17,932 TUs) followed by Russia (20,30,317 TUs) score far above India (10,83,100 TUs). Staff strength-wise only Chinese Railways has more staff than Indian Railways.

Based on the above base data, some Productivity Indices can be derived (Table 3.2).

Table 3.2: Comparative Productivity Indices 2005

Productivity	*India*	*China*	*Russia*	*France*	*Germany*	*S. Africa*
Staff Per Route Km	22.41	26.78	13.63	5.70	6.58	1.63
TU Per Staff	0.76	1.51	1.75	0.71	0.80	3.35
TU Per Route Km	17.07	40.48	23.82	4.03	5.28	5.47

Note: Data pertaining to 2005 has been used due to difficulty in obtaining latest data. This, however, does not affect the essential conclusion of the analysis. With the latest data while the absolute figures may change, there is little chance of change in relative position. Latest data for Indian Railways are in Table 3.3.
Source: Compiled by author

The above Productivity Indices show some expected results and some not so expected ones. China has the highest staff per route kms followed by India and Russia, respectively. Other railways have much lower number of staff per route kms. which reflects much higher level of technological input. Staff Productivity has a lot to do with technical input or in other words infusion of capital. In this sense, a comparison of the Productivity Indices on different railways in relation to capital employed would have been quite interesting. Unfortunately, such a comparison is not possible because of lack of sufficient data. TU per staff is almost the lowest in Indian Railways. The reason for this is not far to seek. It has been estimated that Indian Railways is overstaffed to the extent of 20–25 per cent. What is surprising is the low productivity of staff (TU per staff) in France and Germany. This is unexplainable. The very low TU per route km in France, Germany and South Africa indicates low density of traffic. This is interesting if high technical input (as reflected by low staff per route km) is kept in mind. Does it indicate overcapitalisation?

Evaluative comparison between railways falls in the category of inter-firm comparison, and suffers from the limitations arising out of differences in size, level of technology, traffic mix, work culture, labour laws etc. One example of the wide inherent difference between railways may be seen in the wide difference in their traffic mix (2005).

	India	*China*	*Russia*	*France*	*Germany*	*S. Africa*
PKM/TKM	1.135	0.302	0.093	1.818	1.051	0.009

Thus Indian Railways and French Railways are much more passenger traffic oriented than other railways. Germany is more balanced.

Though not strictly comparable, the wide gulf between Productivity Indices of Indian Railways and other railways is too glaring to be ignored. It should also be viewed in a different light. It indicates the scope for improvement in Indian railways.

Performance of Indian Railways

However, an inter-period comparison of some Productivity Indices of Indian Railways would show whether or not Indian Railways has improved over a period of time.

Table 3.3 shows some interesting trends.

Table 3.3: Productivity Indices on Indian Railways

Description	*1950–51*	*1960–61*	*1970–71*	*1980–81*	*1990–91*	*2000–01*	*2011–12*
Route Km	53596	56247	59790	61240	62367	63028	64600
Staff (000s)	914	1157	1374	1577	1652	1545	1306
PKM (m)	66517	77615	118120	208558	295644	457022	1046522
NTKM (m)	44117	87680	127358	158474	242699	315516	668618
TU (m)	110634	165295	245478	367032	538343	772538	1715140
Product. Indices							
Staff Per Route Km	17.05	20.57	22.98	25.75	26.49	24.51	20.22
TU Per Staff	0.12	0.14	0.18	0.23	0.33	0.50	1.31
TU Per Route Km	2.06	2.94	4.11	5.99	8.63	12.26	26.55

Source: Indian Railway Facts and Figures 2011–12. Productivity Indices are derived.

As seen in Table 3.3, staff per route km increased all along till 2000–01 and then started showing a downward trend. Productivity of staff in terms of TU per staff improved more after 1990–91, which indicates one or both of two factors – better staff management or increased capital input. Actually investments did take a stride from 1990–91 (Table 3.13). Utilisation of infrastructure also improved as reflected by increase in TU per route km.

Chart 3.1: Productivity Indices on Indian Railways

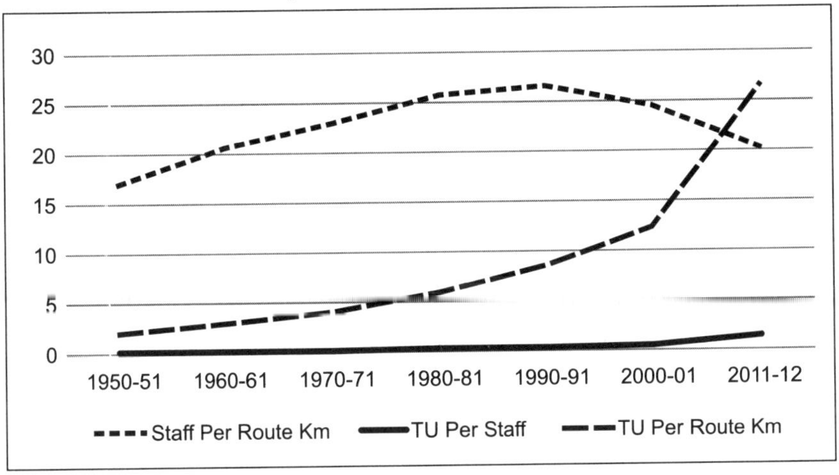

It is rather surprising that staff per route km in 1950–51 was lower than that even in 2011–12 in spite of much technical input in the form of mechanised track maintenance, long welded rails, electric traction, modernised signalling system, better rolling stock, computerisation and so on. In fact, it should have been exactly the opposite. Staff Productivity is discussed in a little more detail subsequently.

Some output indices, asset utilisation indices and some financial indices covering the period 1950–51 to 2011–12 are given below to evaluate the performance of Indian Railways.

Output indices

As mentioned earlier, the output of Indian Railways in terms of earnings consists of 67 per cent from freight and 27 per cent from passengers. Some data showing growth of the two types of traffic from 1950–51 are given as follows.

Freight traffic

The growth both in terms of weight of freight traffic as well as in terms of distance carried is shown in Table 3.4. Freight traffic has grown more than ten times and NTKM by more than 15 times since 1950–51. If we look at the structure of the commodities carried as shown in Table 1.6 in Chapter 1, it is seen that most of the traffic is of the nature of bulk traffic. Only ten commodities accounted for about 90 per cent of the earnings and only three commodities viz. coal, iron ore and cement, which are bulk commodities, accounted for 62 per cent of the earnings. Actually, railways have never been the preferred mode of transport for high rated traffic any time anywhere in the world. High rated freight traffic generally moves by road because of its inherent advantage of flexibility and door-to-door service.

Table 3.4: Freight traffic since 1950–51

Year	*Frt Originating Mill Tonnes*	*Index*	*NTKm Million*	*Index*
1950–51	93	100	44117	100
1960–61	156.2	167.96	87680	198.74
1970–71	196.5	211.29	127358	288.68
1980–81	220	236.56	158474	359.21
1990–91	341.4	367.10	242699	550.13
2000–01	504.2	542.15	315516	715.18
2003–04	581.4	625.16	384074	870.58
2004–05	626.2	673.33	411280	932.25
2005–06	682.4	733.76	441762	1001.34
2006–07	744.56	800.60	483422	1095.77
2007–08	804.11	864.63	523196	1185.93
2008–09	836.61	899.58	552002	1251.22
2009–10	892.22	959.38	601290	1362.94
2010–11	926.43	996.16	626473	1420.03
2011–12	975.16	1048.56	668618	1515.56

Source: Indian Railway Facts and Figures 2011–12

It is, therefore, unrealistic for IR to expect to attract high rated traffic to rail in any major way at least in the foreseeable future. On the contrary, the breakeven point is increasingly shifting in favour of roads due to better highways and better and higher capacity motor vehicles.

Indian Railways must reconcile itself to the international trend of rail being primarily carriers of bulk goods and devise its strategy accordingly.

With the success of the country on the food front, most of the regions of the country have now become more or less self-sufficient in food. This has reduced the need to transport food grains over long distances from Punjab and Haryana to distant parts of the country. Self-sufficiency in food has eliminated the need to import food and move it over longer distances in the hinterland. The fall in imported food traffic has of late been partly made up by import of coal and export of iron ore, which may not last long. Same applies to setting up different kinds of manufacturing facilities all over the country reducing the need to move manufactured goods over long distances. As a result, the Average Lead of Revenue Earning Freight Traffic has been consistently coming down. It has come down from 754 kms in 1980–81 to 689 kms in 2011–12.

It is now short lead traffic which predominates except in the case of bulk goods. This is in the nature of things as seen in other countries as well.

Actually, it is not the share of traffic in terms of percentage which should make railways lose sleep. A higher share of a small cake is no consolation. The percentage fall is inevitable and not important. In the ever-changing dynamics of transport, the main concern of Indian Railways should be with the absolute volume of traffic rather than with the share of traffic. The relevant question for consideration is: whether Indian Railways is in a position, physically, cost-wise, efficiency-wise and quality of service-wise, to handle the traffic the availability of which is quite abundant and which will grow further with economic development.

Going a step further, it is not the absolute volume of traffic alone, but earnings and profits therefrom which should be of concern to railways. It is universally accepted that the very rationale for the existence of a commercial activity is to earn profit. Profit measures everything. It is the crystallised representation of all that is important, except in the case of exploitative monopolistic profit – the demand for the service, quality of service, customer focus, cost and efficiency. Indian Railways is yet to absorb this reality.

Thus, Indian Railways must accept two realities in respect of freight traffic – that it will gradually be pushed to becoming a carrier of long distance bulk goods and that it must strive to earn profit in the commercial sense of the word.

Passenger traffic

During the period 1950–51 and 2011–12 the growth of passenger traffic has been as follows.

Table 3.5: Passenger traffic since 1950–51

Year	*Passengers Millions*	*Index*	*PKM Million*	*Index*
1950–51	1284	100	66517	100
1960–61	1594	124.14	77615	116.68
1970–71	2431	189.33	118120	177.58
1980–81	3613	281.39	208558	313.54
1990–91	3858	300.47	295644	444.46
2000–01	4833	376.40	457022	687.08
2003–04	5112	398.13	541208	813.64
2004–05	5378	418.85	575702	865.50
2005–06	5725	445.87	615614	925.50
2006–07	6219	484.35	694764	1044.49
2007–08	6524	508.10	769956	1157.53
2008–09	6920	538.94	838032	1259.88
2009–10	7246	564.33	903465	1358.25
2010–11	7651	595.87	978508	1471.06
2011–12	8224	640.50	1046522	1573.32

Source: Indian Railway Facts and Figures 2011–12

It is rightly said that for the travelling population of India, Indian Railways is the life-line, at least for those who cannot afford air fare or have to travel long distances or from places not connected by other means of transport. Between the period 1950–51 and 2011–12, the number of passengers increased by more than six times and the number of PKMs by about 16 times, which shows more and more longer distance travel. Indian Railways ran 12,335 passenger trains in 2011–12, perhaps the highest number of trains run by any railway in the world considering the distance involved. In smaller countries, the number of trains may be more. Out of the above number of passengers 53.22 per cent were accounted for by sub-urban traffic and the balance 46.78 per cent by non-suburban traffic. In respect of PKM the sub-urban traffic accounted for 13.77 per cent and the non-suburban traffic 86.23 per cent. Passenger earnings in 2011–12 was ₹ 28,246.43 Crs. of which 6.82 per cent was accounted for by sub-urban traffic and the non-suburban traffic accounted for 93.18 per cent of earnings (Table 1.7).

During the year 2011–12, losses from passenger traffic were to the tune of ₹ 22,500 Crs.

Asset utilisation

Asset utilisation is one area where Indian Railways has acquitted itself rather well, as shown in Table 3.6.

Table 3.6: Freight traffic asset utilisation

Year	*Frt Org Mill Tonnes*	*Index*	*NTKm Million*	*Index*	*Wagons Thousands*	*Index*
1950–51	93.00	100	44117	100	205596	100
1960–61	156.20	167.96	87680	198.74	307907	149.76
1970–71	196.50	211.29	127358	288.68	383990	186.77
1980–81	220.00	236.56	158474	359.21	400946	195.02
1990–91	341.40	367.10	242699	550.13	346102	168.34
2000–01	504.20	542.15	315516	715.18	222193	108.07
2003–04	581.40	625.16	384074	870.58	227752	110.78
2004–05	626.20	673.33	411280	932.25	222409	108.18
2005–06	682.40	733.76	441762	1001.34	207983	101.16
2006–07	744.56	800.60	483422	1095.77	207723	101.03
2007–08	804.11	864.63	523196	1185.93	204034	99.24
2008–09	836.61	899.58	552002	1251.22	212835	103.52
2009–10	892.22	959.38	601290	1362.94	220549	107.27
2010–11	926.43	996.16	626473	1420.03	229997	111.87
2011–12	975.16	1048.56	668618	1515.56	239321	116.40

Source: Indian Railway Facts and Figures 2011–12

While the originating freight in terms of weight went up by more than 10 times and NTKMs went up by 15 times, the number of wagons (in terms of four wheelers) went up only by 1.2 times. This could be achieved only by better utilisation of all freight-related assets such as wagons, locomotives and infrastructure (Chart 3.2).

Chart 3.2: Freight traffic asset utilisation indices

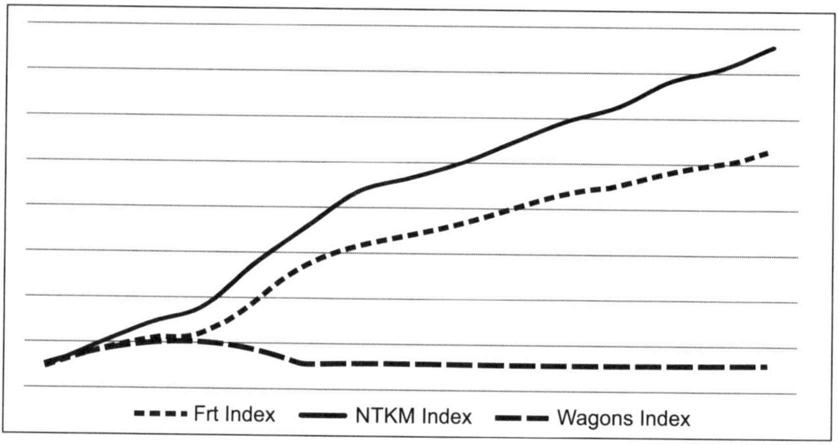

Similar position was obtained with respect to passenger traffic asset utilisation indices (Table 3.7).

Table 3.7: Passenger traffic asset utilisation

Year	*Pass. Coaches Nos.*	*Index*	*Passengers Millions*	*Index*	*PKM Million*	*Index*
1950–51	13022	100	1284	100	66517	100
1960–61	20062	154.06	1594	124.14	77615	116.68
1970–71	24591	188.84	2431	189.33	118120	177.58
1980–81	27410	210.49	3613	281.39	208558	313.54
1990–91	28677	220.22	3858	300.47	295644	444.46
2000–01	33236	255.23	4833	376.40	457022	687.08
2003–04	35654	273.80	5112	398.13	541208	813.64
2004–05	37087	284.80	5378	418.85	575702	865.50
2005–06	38156	293.01	5725	445.87	615614	925.50
2006–07	38855	298.38	6219	484.35	694764	1044.49
2007–08	40696	312.52	6524	508.10	769956	1157.53
2008–09	42079	323.14	6920	538.94	838032	1259.88
2009–10	43526	334.25	7246	564.33	903465	1358.25
2010–11	45048	345.94	7651	595.87	978508	1471.06
2011–12	46688	358.53	8224	640.50	1046522	1573.32

Source: Indian Railway Facts and Figures 2011–12

While the number of coaches increased only by 3.59 times, the number of passengers increased by 6.4 times and the passenger kms increased by 15.7 times (Chart 3.3).

Chart 3.3: Passenger traffic asset utilisation indices

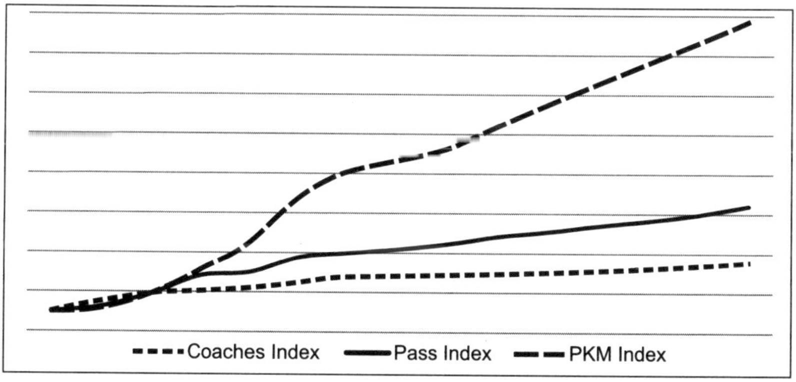

Table 3.8 links increase in investment on different types of assets to increase in output.

Table 3.8: Indices of growth of traffic output and inputs

Year	*Traffic Output Indices*			*Investment Input Indices*			
	Frt Tfc Ntkm	*Pass Tfc Non-sub PKM*	*Wagon Capacity*	*Passenger Coaches*	*Route Kms*	*Running Track Kms*	*Tractive Effort of Locos*
1950–51	100	100	100	100	100	100	100
1960–61	199	110	152	154	105	107	144
1970–71	289	159	226	188	112	121	178
1980–81	359	279	269	210	114	128	201
1990–91	550	394	278	219	116	133	192
2000–01	715	614	246	254	118	138	233
2007–08	1185	1085	247	311	118	144	292
2008–09	1251	1189	283	321	119	147	310
2009–10	1363	1288	278	332	119	147	322
2010–11	1420	1403	294	344	120	147	343
2011–12	1516	1505	311	356	121	151	371

Source: Compiled by author

It will be seen that in 2011–12 while investment inputs increased between 1.2 times in route kms to 3.71 times in Tractive Effort of Locomotives, the increase in output indices was 15 times both in NTKM and in non-suburban PKM. This shows all-round improvement in utilisation of passenger coaches and other assets.

More such data on asset utilisation such as Wagon Utilisation, Engine Utilisation, Route Utilisation are available in Indian Railway Year Book, Statistical Summary, Annual Statistics and other statistical publications of Indian Railways. Further statistics on this are not being given.

The above discussion does indicate more intensive utilisation of assets and improved performance over the years. Whether it could have been better is impossible to say.

Staff productivity

The index of staff productivity for the last thirty years does show some improvement (Table 3.9).

Table 3.9: Staff productivity on Indian Railways (₹ Crs)

Year	*Emp (000s)*	*TU(000) Per Emp*	*Index*	*Tot Inv*	*Index*	*Inv per 000 Emp*	*Index*
1980–81	1572.2	232	100	7448	100	4.7	100
1990–91	1651.8	325	140	22201	298	13.4	284
2000–01	1545.3	500	216	63341	850	41.0	865
2010–11	1332.0	1205	519	231615	3110	173.9	3670
2011–12	1305.7	1313	566	257958	3463	197.6	4170

Source: Compiled by author

But staff productivity is closely linked to capital investment. If this is taken into account staff productivity presents a very dismal picture. While capital investment per employee increased by more than 42 times (197.6/4.7), the productivity per staff increased only by 5.6 times (1313/232). The gap is too wide to be explained by any factor other than excessive overstaffing and non-productive investments. Inflation may account for part of it but not entirely. For example, almost five times increase in Investment per thousand employees between 2000–01 and 2011–12 cannot be explained by inflation alone.

A comparison with some other countries does not show Indian Railways in very positive light (Chart 3.4).

Chart 3.4: Comparative staff productivity

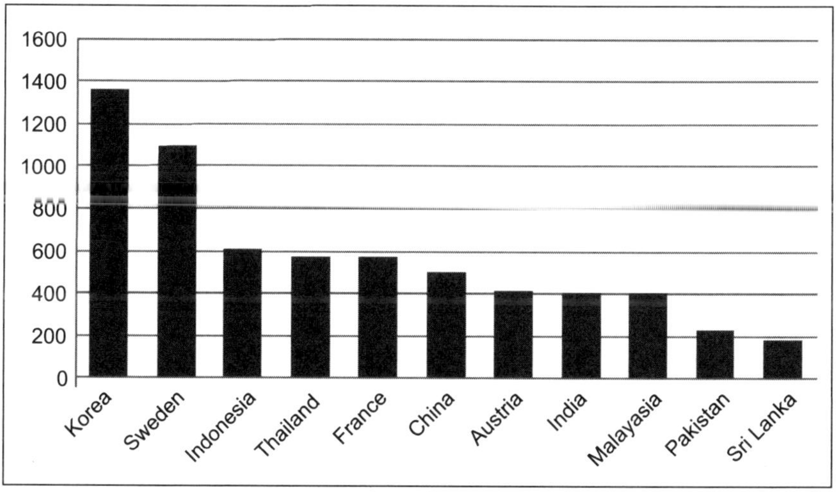

Note: Productivity in Thousand TU/Per Employee. TU=PKM+TKM
Source: Expert Group on Indian Railways, 'The Indian Railway Report; Policy Imperatives for Reinvention and Growth' National council of Applied Economic Research, India 2001, 131

The productivity of staff in Indian Railways ranks lower than even such countries as Indonesia, Thailand and Malaysia who would perhaps be similarly or even worse placed, as far as technology is concerned.

If the physical performance of Indian Railways has failed on any front, it is the staff front. The level of excess staff on Indian Railways is generally estimated to be around 25 per cent or so.

Financial performance

As shown above, in terms of inter-period comparison, Indian Railways has not done too badly in respect of physical performance, except in indices related to staff. The volume of traffic handled has increased quite substantially compared to the inputs during the period. Utilisation of assets has also improved. Whether the same can be said of its financial performance is not so certain.

The financial results for the year 2011–12 in Table 1.10 give some idea of the finances of Indian Railways.

Although the Railways were able to pay the Dividend in 2011–12, it left very little surplus for expenditure on works of capital nature financed out of internal resources and meeting other obligations. After meeting the working expenses, a surplus of only ₹5.15 per ₹100 of revenue was available to pay Dividend, contribution to state governments for safety works on railway tracks (spent mostly on level crossing gates and road over bridges), and appropriation to Development Fund, Safety Fund and Capital Fund. As can be appreciated, this meagre surplus is totally inadequate, to say the least. Further, during the same period:

- Development Fund opened with a negative balance of ₹ 1213.34 Crs. and had to borrow ₹ 3000 Crs. from the general revenue for works to be executed from this fund.
- DRF opened with a negative balance of ₹ 33.54 Crs.
- Capital Fund opened with a negative balance of ₹ 885.71 Crs. and closed with a negative balance of ₹ 401.53 Crs. No work could be executed from this fund during the year for want of funds.

[*Source*: Explanatory Memorandum on the Railway Budget for 2013–14]

The above figures present only a one-year snap-shot picture.

There are two other important statistics which further highlight the financial scenario viz. the OR and the ability of Indian Railways to pay Dividend to the General Revenue over a period of time. The OR of Indian Railways for the last ten years is given in Table 3.10.

Table 3.10: Operating Ratio since 2000–01

Year	*OR*
2000–01	98.34
2003–04	92.13
2004–05	90.98
2005–06	83.72
2006–07	78.68
2007–08	75.94
2008–09	90.46
2009–10	96.28
2010–11	94.59
2011–12	94.85

Source: Explanatory Memorandum on the Railway Budget 2013–14

With the exception of three years 2005–06, 2006–07 and 2007–08, the OR has been consistently in the nineties.

It needs to be kept in mind that the above figures of OR are not totally objective. This is because the Appropriation to DRF, which forms a part of total working expenditure, is not based on any objective principle. It can be increased or decreased depending upon the financial position during the year. Thus, if it is desired to show a better OR, one only needs to reduce the Appropriation to DRF. Therefore, it is impossible to say what would have been the position of OR, if Appropriation to DRF had been based on some objective principle. Hopefully this issue will get addressed when the reform of railway accounts, which is already underway, is completed.

For quite some time it has been advocated that railway accounts which is a curious mixture of government accounting system and commercial accounting system should be recast on commercial accounting standards to give a clearer picture of railway finances. This is still to be implemented. However, the Rakesh Mohan Committee made an attempt to do so for the financial year 2000–01. Exhibit 5.6 of the report is reproduced in Table 3.11.

Table 3.11: Comparison of railway profitability (2000–2001) (₹ Crs)

As presented by Railway		*In Commercial Practice*		*Remarks*
Particulars	*Amount*	*Amount*	*Particular*	
Capital Investment	43,198			Total of Capital at Charge (32,500) and Investment from Capital Fund (10,698)
		49,188	Capital Employed	Total of Equity Capital (8,198), Preference Capital (16,396) and Long Term Debt (24,594) in restructured Railway Capital
Gross Traffic Receipts	36,529	35,112	Traffic Earnings	'Sundry Other Income' (1417) included in Railway presentation but shown separately (below) in Commercial format
			Other Income	
		717	Sundry Income	Breakup of 'Sundry Other Income' shown in the Commercial format

Contd.

Contd.

As presented by Railway		*In Commercial Practice*		*Remarks*
Particulars	*Amount*	*Amount*	*Particular*	
		700	From Non-conventional Sources	
		815	Miscellaneous Receipts	This item appears as 'Net Misc. Receipts' in the Railway presentation (see below)
		37,344	Total Income	
Ordinary Working Expense	28,115	25,051	Total Expenses	Lease Charges to IRFC (3064) excluded in the Commercial format, this item is adjusted against 'Interest Charges' on total debt
Appropriation to Funds		12,293	Operating Surplus	Total Income less Total Expenses
Depreciation Reserve Fund	2,441			'Depreciation' as actually 'accrued' taken as deduction from Earnings in the Commercial format (see below)
Pension Fund	4,996	5,314	Pension Outgo	Actual Outgo as budgeted shown in the Commercial format
Net Traffic Receipts	977	6,979	Earnings Before Interest Tax & Depreciation (EBITDA)	Net of Ordinary Working Expenses and appropriation to Funds in Railway presentation; Operating Surplus less Pension Outgo in Commercial format
		4,190	Depreciation	As 'accrued' on restructured capital
Net Miscellaneous Receipts	815			Includes Dividend Rebate; already taken as part of Total Income in Commercial format
		2,789	Earnings Before Interest and Tax (EBIT)	EBITDA less Depreciation

Contd.

Contd.

As presented by Railway		*In Commercial Practice*		*Remarks*
Particulars	*Amount*	*Amount*	*Particular*	
		2,951	Interest & Finance charges	Calculated liability for 2000–01 in restructured accounts
Net Revenue	1,792	-162	Profit Before Tax (PBT)	Net Traffic Receipts plus Net Miscellaneous Receipts in Railway presentation; EBIT less Interest & Finance charges in Commercial format
		0	Tax	No tax liability for railway; 'zero' tax assumed in restructured model.
		-162	Profit After Tax (PAT)	Same as PBT because 'zero' tax assumed.
Total Dividend Payable	2,115			Dividend as accrued in present railway: Government arrangements
Surplus (Deficit) after paying Dividend	-323			Loan on Dividend account (1500) ignored in this presentation
Ratio of 'Net Revenue' to 'Capital at Charge' and investment from Capital Fund (Percent)	4			Ratio to 'Capital Investment' as defined in railway presentation
		5.7	Return on Capital Employed (Percent)	Ratio of EBIT to 'Capital Employed' in Commercial presentation

Note: Common figures as in Railway Budget Estimate 2000–01.
Source: Expert Group on Indian Railways, 'The Indian Railway Report: Policy Imperatives for Reinvention and Growth' National Council of Applied Economic Research, India 2001, 297

It will be seen that the Net Revenue of ₹ 1,792 Crs as currently calculated by Railways converts to a PBT deficit of ₹ 162 Crs. when the financial data are recast on commercial accounting principles.

Further, even under the present system of accounting and with the handle of subjective adjustability of Appropriation to DRF, the picture regarding payment of Dividend is quite disturbing. For a number of years, Indian Railways has been unable to pay the full amount of Dividend to the government. It could pay only in parts and had to defer the payment of the balance amount (Table 3.12).

Table 3.12: Deferred Dividend liability (₹ Crs.)

Year	*Amount*
1978–79	Nil
1979–80	66.24
1980–81	264.11
1981–82	264.11
1982–83	266.11
1983–84	308.86
1984–85	504.45
1985–86	428.43
1986–87	428.43
1987–88	428.43
1988–89	428.43
1989–90	428.43
1990–91	428.43
1991–92	428.43
1992–93	428.43
1993–94	428.43
1994–95	416.46
1995–96	341.99
1996–97	Nil
1997–98	Nil
1998–99	Nil
1999–2000	Nil
2000–01	1823.3
2001–02	2823.3
2002–03	2773.3
2003–04	2473.3
2004–05	1990
2005–06	1327
2006–07	664
2007–08	Nil

Source: Explanatory Memorandum on the Railway Budget for 2013–14

The deferred liability persisted right from 1979–80 (with the exception of a few years) and could be cleared only in 2007–08. If a commercial entity is not able to pay interest on borrowed capital, it can certainly not be said to be in pink of health. This is in spite of the reduced rate of Dividend being as low as 3.5 to 4 per cent (after allowing for concessions in the calculation of Dividend).

During the very same years when Railways was not able to pay Dividend, it paid bonus to its employees. A more detailed discussion on this subject is in Chapter 12 on 'Incentive Scheme'.

Indian Railways measures its productivity of capital by relating Net Revenue to capital-at-charge (Table 3.13).

Table 3.13: Productivity of capital

Year	*Capital at charge ₹ Cr.*	*Total Investment ₹ Cr.*	*Net Revenue ₹ Cr*	*% Net Rev/ to Capital-at-Chg*	*% Net Rev/ Total Inves.*
1950–51	855.2	855.2	47.56	5.75	5.56
1960–61	1520.9	1868.6	87.87	5.77	4.70
1970–71	3330.3	4099.4	144.73	4.35	3.53
1980–81	6096.3	7448.4	127.49	2.09	1.71
1990–91	16125.8	22200.5	1113.78	6.91	5.02
2000–01	43051.88	63341.01	1071.23	2.49	1.69
2003–04	56061.79	87474.5	4478.49	7.99	5.12
2004–05	59346.93	98490.02	5273.55	8.89	5.35
2005–06	65878.37	112180.41	8005.88	12.15	7.14
2006–07	76030.69	130168.71	14453.13	19.01	11.10
2007–08	88521.14	151434.35	18334.02	20.71	12.11
2008–09	104301.25	176726.41	9174.45	9.8	5.19
2009–10	123000.69	203315.37	5544.09	4.51	2.73
2010–11	143220.57	231615.25	6346.14	4.43	2.74
2011–12	161447.97	257958.35	6781.6	4.2	2.63

Source: Explanatory Memorandum on the Railway Budget 2013–14.

Relating Net Revenue to capital-at-charge may have been justified at one time when loan capital from the government formed the dominant part of investments. It is not so any more. In the year 2011–12, it formed only 62.59 per cent of total investment (161447.97x100/257958.35). This percentage is expected to fall further as Indian Railways has to increasingly depend on borrowed capital at commercial rates for future investments. Therefore, it would be more in fitness of things to relate Net Revenue to total investment. However, whatever one relates it to, the ratio is rather poor except in a couple of years. In 2011–12 the ratio of Net Revenue to capital-at-charge was 4.2 and the ratio in relation to total investment was 2.3. It must be kept in mind that if the Appropriation to DRF had been based on an objective principle (thereby affecting Net Revenue) the above productivity ratios could have been quite different. This is completely unsustainable.

The graph below shows the relationship between Net Revenue to both capital-at-charge and total investment. Both are almost touching the X-axis for most of the years.

Chart 3.5: Productivity of investments

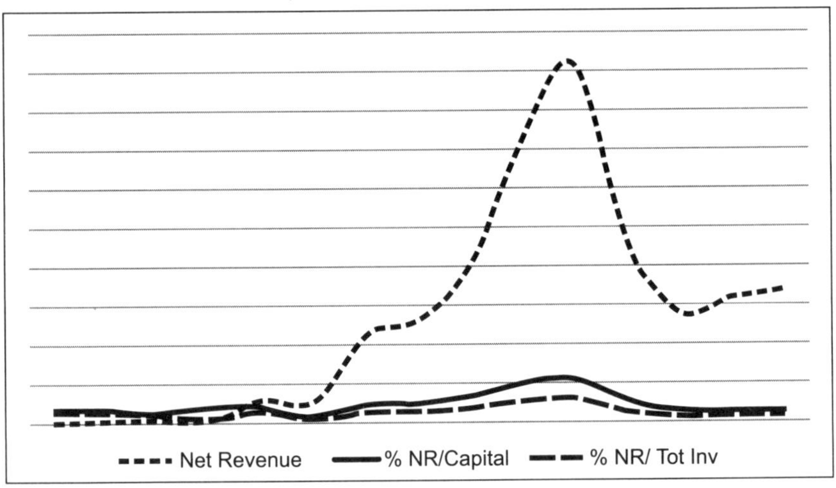

Note: NR is Net Revenue

The above analysis indicates that as far as performance is concerned, the main failure of Indian Railways has been more on the financial side rather than on the physical side.

Add to the above the fact that IR has been able to add only 11,004 kms to its route length since 1950–51 in spite of additional investment of ₹ 257,103.35

Crs. Its share of total traffic has been falling, quality of service leaves much to be desired and its safety record has been the subject of criticism. But these are only the symptoms of the problem. What causes them is the real concern.

The causes are both external and internal to the organisation.

The external factors are basically two – (i) all-pervasive political and government bureaucratic interference/control in the working of railways and (ii) failure to accept that railway is actually a commercial undertaking like any other business.

The external factors have had a strong bearing on the internal factors as well. All the internal factors can be summarised in four words 'absence of commercial culture'. As long as Indian Railways remains a government department and a commercial-cum-public utility service such that a bail-out can always be expected without repercussion on individual fortunes, it is hard to see why anyone should put in extra effort. Further, the very dual character of Indian Railways both as a commercial undertaking and as a public utility service confuses the aim of the organisation. These external influences affect all important aspects of railway working – be it investment decisions, introduction of new trains, tariff policy, staff strength, running of uneconomic services, transfers and promotions in senior positions and what have you.

IR also must accept its share of failure, to do what it can on its own to make Indian Railways a more productive organisation. For example, lack of professionalism and ad-hocism in manning its most important administrative positions such as that of the Divisional Railway Managers, General Managers and the Chairman Railway Board, relegating the commercial function to secondary importance, having a faulty incentive scheme and so on.

These are problems of systemic nature and call for systemic reforms.

Part 2

The Reform Wave

4

Introduction

Different railways of the world have had different origins. Some originated as private railways as in India and the United Kingdom while others originated as government railways as in Sweden and there were private as well as government owned railways as in Japan. But by 1950s, all of them had become fully government-owned vertically integrated railways. And they faced remarkably similar problems – increasing competition from road, political interference, excess staff, monopolistic tendencies, hostile labour, management indifference, lack of incentive to perform, acute financial problems, mounting debt etc. In fact, by the end of the 1970s railways had come to be regarded as a sunset industry. At the same time the potentialities of railways were also recognised – the only mode of transport capable of transporting bulk goods or passengers over long distances, ideal for concentrated suburban local passenger traffic, least polluting, least cost over long distances etc. It was also recognised that railways were unfairly pitted against road. Unlike road they had to bear the cost of infrastructure as well. Thus, by the middle of the 1980s, as if on a cue, there was sudden awakening and a wave of reforms followed. Many governments started reforming their railways – Japan, Sweden, United Kingdom, France, Germany, New Zealand, Australia, Argentina, Brazil, Mexico and more recently Russia and China.

There was a sort of rediscovery of railways. In the context of railways, reform implied changing the existing structure of railways and the relationship between government and railways such that railways could work in the same economic environment as road. They are not made to bear the cost of infrastructure, are allowed to work as any commercial enterprise and are not made to bear the cost of Public Service Obligations which are actually the responsibility of the state. All reform measures were aimed at making railways financially self-sufficient. The path adopted by different railways differed depending on their history, culture, social needs, local conditions, traffic mix, strategic requirements, political compulsions and financial conditions of the government.

However, there were some commonalities in the reasons for reform as well as the structures developed.

- In all cases, mounting financial losses of the railways and the inability of the governments to continue to shoulder their burden provided the trigger for reforms. It was recognised that railways cannot be allowed to fail because of their socio-economic importance. No other mode of transport could substitute the role of railways.
- It was recognised that railways were, in fact, commercial entities and must be allowed to be run as such. This could be done only by creating arms-length relationship between government and railways.
- Railways are a very capital-intensive industry. And traffic cannot bear the full cost of railways, particularly infrastructure cost. Therefore, all governments fully or partially relieved railways of the burden of capital cost of rail infrastructure in some way.
- Additional assistance was provided to railways in different ways such as – relieving railways of their debt burden and excess staff, compensating railways for losses on unprofitable services required by the government in furtherance of their public services obligations etc.

In what follows, an attempt has been made to describe the important elements of reforms in three railways – Japan, Sweden and United Kingdom in some detail and a brief summary of reforms in Russian Railways, German Railways and Chinese Railways. Only Japan, Sweden and United Kingdom have been discussed in more detail than other railways because taken together they contain all the elements and patterns of reforms adopted by other railways. The British response is actually a combination of Japanese and Swedish structures. The Swedish model has been adopted by the European Union and has been followed by many other countries such as Russia, Germany and France in varying degrees.

Some South American and Latin American countries followed a much different route. They allowed concession to different parts of their railways for different periods of time varying from seventy years to ninety years. This approach is not discussed here as the chances of its applicability in Indian

Railways, at least in foreseeable future, are extremely remote. Actually, the concept of concessioning to itself is yet to strike root in India whether in railways or in any other sector.

The description of reforms in other railways may not be fully up to date for want of up-to-date published material. The process of churning also has not yet stabilised in any country. However, this does not affect the main theme of this book. What is of interest to us is the institutional structures which were created, to see whether they could be suitable for Indian conditions or whether at least certain aspects of those structures could be of use to Indian Railways. In this respect, one can make do without the latest changes without much loss. However, it is highly unlikely that fundamentals of the structures would have changed drastically except perhaps in Britain where the structure is so complex and volatile that major changes are not ruled out even in the short run, so much so that at present there is strong demand for renationalisation of railways in Britain.

5

Japanese Railways

Japan was the first country in the world to embark on reform of its railways in 1987. Some say that the process is still continuing as some of the Japanese Railways (JR) have still to be sold off. However, unlike some other countries, the reform in Japanese Railways is generally considered a success story.

The Railway lines were first constructed in Japan in 1872, i.e., nineteen years after India. By 1981, the Japanese National Railways (JNR) operated 21,418 kms of truck. In addition, more than 5000 kms were owned and operated by private railways. The private railways mainly operated commuter lines. Some basic data about JNR before reforms and after reforms is given in Table 5.1.

Table 5.1: Japanese Railways

Item	*1987*	*1992*
Track Kms. (TKU)	29,987	28,461
NTKM (M)	20,000	26,219
PKM (M)	204,679	249,603
No. of Freight Cars	30,753	28,886
No. of Pass. Cars	2,852	2,065
Tfc. Mix (PKM/TU) %age	91.1	90.6
NTKM+PKM per TKM	10.6	13.5
NTKM+PKM per emp.	1,125	1,428
Total Emp.	199,740	193,196
Operating Ratio	96	80.1

Source: Ron Kapicki and Louis S. Thompson, 'Best Methods of Railway Restructuring and Privatization'

Some facts about Japan and Japanese Railways are relevant. Railways in Japan have a very small share in total transport business of the country. In 1990, Railways held only 5 per cent of the total transport market. About 50 per cent of the transport business was held by highways and 45 per cent by coastal shipping. Most of the bulk goods moved by coastal shipping and finished goods by road. Further, in the railway sector itself, it is the passenger traffic which overwhelmingly predominates. The reason for this is obvious. The population in Japan is highly concentrated in about 20 per cent of the land and is spread along the railway lines. The highest concentration is around three cities – Tokyo, Nagoya and Osaka. Therefore, there is predominance of short distance commuter traffic. Since Japan is a small country with good air connections, the long distance passenger traffic is rather small, largely on the Shinkansen routes. Thus, as far as role models go, there cannot be more dissimilar models than Japanese Railways and Indian Railways.

The JNR faced strong competition for passenger traffic from more than a hundred private railway companies operating railway lines parallel to JNR lines. But unlike JNR, the private railways not only run railway passenger services, they had also diversified into other related businesses such as real estate, hotels, amusement parks, retail etc. with the intention of attracting as much passenger traffic as possible to their railways and earning revenues from other activities. In some private railway companies earnings from other business activities far exceeded their earnings from railways.

Prior to 1949, JNR was a fully government-owned departmental undertaking. In 1949, it was converted into a government-owned Corporation. But since it was government owned, even as a corporation it did not have much freedom of decision.

- All important decisions such as pricing, investment, wages, employment of top officials etc. continued to remain with the government and thus subject to political influence.
- JNR budget was approved by the Diet including tariffs.
- It continued to shoulder a number of public service objectives of the government including operating low density non-economic lines.
- While JNR's competitors, i.e., the private railways could engage in any business which they found profitable, JNR was restricted to rail transport business only.

In addition to the above-mentioned external factors, JNR suffered from some debilitating internal problems as well, such as

- It was heavily overstaffed. For a track length of approximately 30,000 kms it employed 224,000 persons i.e., 7.5 persons per track kms. Compare this figure pertaining to the year 1986 with 11.6 persons in Indian Railways today (2013) even with difference in technical input.
- Assured of government bail-out, JNR management lacked compelling motivation to improve matters. The management was slow to react to challenges from the competitors. Comparison with IR is again warranted.
- JNR management faced strong and adversarial trade union.
- The labour unions were completely isolated from, and thus indifferent to, the financial performance of the railways. This bears uncanny resemblance to the Productivity Linked Bonus scheme in Indian Railways which is discussed in detail in Chapter 12 on 'Incentive Scheme'.
- There was no incentive structure to award performance by way of linking incentive to performance.
- Due to continuing non-cooperative attitude of labour and bad financial performance, JNR management too had become demoralised and disinterested.

Over the period 1970–87, both internal and external factors contributed to JNR's performance difficulties. The internal causes cited by the Ad Hoc Commission on Administrative Reforms of JNR were (1) too much government interference (2) unclear management responsibilities that were subject to frequently conflicting pressures from different stakeholders (3) a labour-management relationship that was characterised by an adversarial union and very high wage levels and (4) limitations on the ability to pursue varied and dynamic business activities.[1]

The situation was made worse by technological advances in alternative modes of transport and improvements in related infrastructure such as highways and airways.

All the above symptoms closely resemble the situation prevailing in Indian Railways today.

---

[1] Ron Kopicki and Louis S. Thompson, 'Best Methods of Railway Restructuring and Privatisation', World Bank, 75.

These factors adversely affected the financial performance of JNR and in 1964, for the first time JNR incurred operating loss. The position continued to deteriorate. In 1986, JNR incurred loss to the tune of $20 billion in spite of annual subsidy to the extent of $50 billion. The losses were financed through Bonds guaranteed by the government. By the year 1987, the cumulative losses of JNR amounted to more than $300 billion. JNR was in no position to pay even the interest on the bonds in spite of receiving annual subsidy of $50 billion from the government.

Further, by the end of the 1970s, the Japanese economy had fallen into in distress. Therefore, in 1981, the newly elected government of Prime Minister Suzuki appointed a high-level committee called 'Provisional Committee on Administrative Reforms' headed by Mr Toshio Doko, a well-regarded industrialist, to look into the affairs of the economy and recommend measures to improve it. The Committee submitted its report in 1981. It recommended privatisation of three major government-owned companies – Japan National Railways, Japan Monopoly Corporation (Tobacco and Salt) and Nippon Telegraph and Telephone Public Corporation. Regarding JNR it said that restoring JNR's financial health would be impossible as long as the railway was operated as a centralised, nationwide public corporation and suggested appointment of a supervisory committee for restructuring JNR. This led to setting up the Supervisory Committee for the reconstruction of JNR.

> The Supervising Committee for Reconstruction of JNR began its work in 1983 and completed it in April 1987. Though initially there was vehement opposition from JNR management, labour unions, some politicians and also academicians, it was ultimately decided to privatise JNR and make over its ownership to private individuals. The privatisation of JNR was accomplished in three stages - first reorganization, then economic recuperation, and finally privatization.[2]

As a part of reorganisation, JNR was dissolved as a corporation and seven new joint stock companies were created in its place, jointly called the JR group companies – six passenger companies and one freight company. Of the six passenger companies three were on the main island of Honshu viz. JR East centred around Tokyo, JR West centred around Osaka and JR Central based in Nagoya. There were three other passenger companies on smaller islands viz.

[2] Ron Kopicki and Louis S. Thompson, 'Best Methods of Railway Restructuring and Privatisation', World Bank.

JR Hokkaido, JR Shikoku and JR Kyushu. There was one freight company called JR Freight. Thus, all railway companies, except for JR freight, were basically regional railways.

Freight operation was not seen as a profitable proposition because of extremely keen competition from road for manufactured goods and coastal shipping for raw material. Therefore, freight was kept separate from passenger railways so that the losses in freight do not tell upon the good work of the passenger railways and hamper their initiative and dynamism in dealing with passenger traffic.

> Were JR Freight to remain within the fold of the passenger JRs, it was feared that managerial responsibility for its losses would be vague and its poor performance would damage the morale and the good results the healthier passenger companies were bound to achieve.[3]

An important consideration in carving out passenger regions was that a region should be such that about 95 per cent of the journeys commence and be completed within the region itself. This became possible because of predominant commuter traffic. The un-economic rural lines falling within the geographical region of a railway company were attached with the railway of that region. Each JR passenger railway became the owner of the railway lines and related infrastructure falling within its jurisdiction and owner of its rolling stock. It was responsible for and had the monopoly of train operation in its region. Trains of other regions could also ply on the regions of other JRs on payment of access charges. Thus, each JR was a vertically integrated railway system except for JR freight.

JR Freight did not own any infrastructure. It could operate on any region by paying access charges. However, since freight was not expected to be able to bear its cost, the access charges were kept very low. It was required to pay only the avoidable cost to passenger railways which included only such costs as additional maintenance required to be carried out by the passenger railways as a result of running the freight train, additional electricity cost etc. As obvious, the access charge so worked out amounted to practically nothing.

---

[3] Fumitoshi Mizutani and Kiyoshi Nakumara, 'The Japanese Experience with Railway Restructuring', Governance, Regulation and Privatisation in Asia-Pacific Region, NBER East Asia Seminar on Economics, Volume 12, University of Chicago Press, January 2004.

Simultaneously, a Japan National Railway Settlement Corporation (JNRSC) was set up which became the holding company for all the newly created JR companies. The Settlement Corporation was a temporary organisation. It was set up with an express purpose and was to be wound up on completion of that purpose. It became the owner of all the shares of all the JR companies. The main tasks of the Corporation were:

- To take over the debt of JNR amounting to more than $300 billion. About 40 per cent of the debt was allocated to the three passenger JR companies on the main island as it was felt that they could bear this burden and the balance 60 per cent was taken over by the Settlement Corporation. The debt was to be liquidated by the Settlement Corporation by sale of real estate, other redundant assets of JNR and the sale of shares of JR companies to public. A small part of it was to be borne by the taxpayers.
- To redeploy or otherwise resettle the surplus staff of JNR.
- To ensure enlisting of JR companies with Tokyo Stock Exchange and subsequent sale of its shares.

The Supervisory Committee had estimated that JNR had 93,000 surplus staff. By 1 April 1987 it had been possible to retire, redeploy a large number of employees and about 23,000 only were transferred to the Settlement Corporation. By this time, the Japanese economy had regained its buoyancy and thus enabled large-scale absorption of surplus staff of JNR along with redeployment in local governments, the police department and other government-owned companies. Those who could not be redeployed were given generous voluntary retirement benefits.

It was foreseen that while the three railways on the main island viz. JR East, JR West and JR central had the potential to become profitable, the three passenger lines on the smaller islands and JR freight did not have such potential.

The main aim of the Supervisory Committee was to take all steps to create such organisations which could compete with road and also be profitable enough to stand on their own legs such that they could in time be listed on the Tokyo Stock Exchange and their shares could ultimately be sold to the public. Therefore, a number of steps were taken specifically to improve the financial conditions of the JR companies.

Since the three railways in smaller islands were not expected to meet costs, a complex system of subsidising them was developed. A Management

Stabilisation Fund (MSF) was created with a lump sum grant (1,278 billion yen) from the JNR Settlement Corporation. Interest earned on this Fund was to be utilised for subsidising the operating losses of the island railways. However, due to the fall in market interest rate, the interest earned on the Fund proved to be inadequate. Hence, a new scheme was formulated according to which the Corporation for Advanced Transport and Technology (CATT) borrowed a part of the MSF at fixed interest rate of 4.99 per cent which was higher than the market rate. This scheme was scheduled to be closed in 2001 but was extended up to 2006.

Although the restructuring of JNR was completed in 1987, it was not before 1993 that shares of any JR company could be offered for sale to the public. JR East was the first company to do this in September 1993 followed by JR West.

Features of JNR restructuring

- The reform was triggered by acute financial distress of JNR with debt totalling more than $300 billion and increasing every year.
- There was political commitment to treat railways as a commercial enterprise. And it was realised that a commercial enterprise cannot work successfully in a government-type set-up. Therefore, deliberate attempt was made to create a complete arms-length distance between the government and railways. Right from the beginning, full privatisation of ownership of railways was the aim.
- A mixed structure of railways was adopted. For passenger traffic a geographically separated and vertically integrated approach was followed while for JR Freight a vertically separated but geographically integrated approach was followed.
- A separate agency viz. the JNR Resettlement Corporation was created to take over the burdens of JNR. The Settlement Corporation relieved the JRs not only of the huge debt of JNR but also of surplus staff.
- Passenger JRs thus started with a clean slate. This was done with the express intention of enabling them to compete not only with road but also with private railways.
- Passenger JRs were permitted to undertake other non-railway commercial activities.

- The commercial nature of operations was emphasised. The JR Boards set up performance targets in terms of profit and, borrowing the idea from the private sector, devised management incentives in relation to performance. This point needs to be specially noted. It is made use of in the proposed incentive scheme for Indian Railways in Chapter 12.
- However, some government control did remain. The company Plans and the appointment of company Directors still required the approval of the Minister of Land, Infrastructure and Transport.

How successful?

Restructuring of JNR is considered fairly successful. The performance of passenger railways has improved not only in respect of volume and quality of service but financially as well. While earlier the government had to provide a subsidy of $50 billion every year to JNR, it now receives more than $6 billion per year by way of taxes from the JR companies.

> However, although many people believe that the 1987 rail reform was a success, it is only the three major passenger companies that achieved true privatization; the other three passenger companies (JR Hokkaido, JR Shikoku and JR Kyushu) and the freight company (JR Freight) still fall far short of true privatization. These smaller companies only narrowly avoid falling into red, thanks to a complex financial support system.[4]

Further,

> ... the current Japanese Railways show two different aspects i.e. the prosperous three major passenger companies and four other companies struggling for existence, the success of the former group is too much highlighted and the difficulties of the latter are too often neglected.[5]

Besides the determined effort of the Japanese government to do everything possible to make the Railways commercially successful, there were some external factors also which aided the success of JNR restructuring.

---

[4] Tatsuhiko Suga, '20 Years After JNR Privatisation A Bird's-Eye View of World Railway Reform Trends', *Japan Railway & Transport Review No. 47.*

[5] Tatsuhiko Suga, '20 Years After JNR Privatisation A Bird's-Eye View of World Railway Reform Trends', *Japan Railway & Transport Review No. 47.*

- The three major passenger JRs on the main island found very strong ready-made market in the form of extremely high commuter traffic.
- JR companies started with a rather clean slate in respect of debt and surplus staff.
- The passenger companies inherited highly technically superior infrastructure and rolling stock from JNR without bearing the cost of debt which the erstwhile JNR had to raise to create them. In fact,

> ... the newly founded JR companies have saved a lot of money so far, by limiting their investments to the lowest level.[6]

This enabled the JR companies to keep their maintenance costs also low.

- The recovery of JR was no less aided by buoyancy in the Japanese economy. It directly aided the redeployment of surplus staff.

However, the shares of passenger JRs could not be offered for sale for long. JR East was the first company to be put on sale. 62.5 per cent of its shares were offered in the Tokyo Stock Exchange in 1993. Thus, in spite of all the favourable factors, it took seven years to bring JR East to a state when it was felt that its share could be found attractive by common man. The shares were heavily oversubscribed. JR East was followed by JR West in 1996 and JR Central in 1997.

> As of June 2002, all of JR East, 68.3% of JR West's, and 60.4% of JR Central's shares were held by private sector. All shares of other four JR companies, however, are still held by the government. ... In conclusion, the Japanese approach to rail restructuring has succeeded in many ways, by improving productivity, cutting operating deficits, decreasing fares, and providing better services.[7]

---

[6] Tatsuhiko Suga, '20 Years After JNR Privatisation A Bird's-Eye View of World Railway Reform Trends', *Japan Railway & Transport Review No. 47.*

[7] Fumitoshi Mizutani and Kiyoshi Nakumara, 'The Japanese Experience with Railway Restructuring', Governance, Regulation and Privatisation in Asia-Pacific Region, NBER East Asia Seminar on Economics, Volume 12, University of Chicago Press, January 2004.

6

Swedish Railways

Sweden reformed its railways in 1988, soon after Japan. However, the process had started much earlier. Unlike Japan or United Kingdom where it was done at one stroke, in Sweden it proceeded in a series of steps through a slew of legislative measures.

Following are some basic statistics of Swedish Railways (Table 6.1):

Table 6.1: Swedish Railways

Item	*1992*
Track Kms.	17,114
NTKM (000,000)	19,202
Net PKM (000,000)	5,234
No. of Freight Cars	23,543
No. of Paasenger Cars	1,063
Tfc Mix (PKM as % of TU)	21.3
No. of Employees	24,943
OR	94

Source: Ron Kapicki & Louis S. Thompson 'Best Methods of Railway Restructuring and Privatization

All in all, there are about 500 railway stations where trains stop for passengers. Many of these are very simple stops (controlled by Banverket), with no special buildings or facilities for passengers. Many stations (with or without passenger facilities) are owned and maintained by regional authorities, being used only for local and regional services. About 170 stations are equipped with station buildings on separate estates.[1]

---

[1] G. Alexandersson and S. Hulten, 'The Swedish Railway Deregulation Path', *Review of Network Economics*, Vol 7, 1 March 2008.

It would be interesting to compare this with facilities at stations on Indian Railways and the constant demand for additional facilities.

Construction of railways in Sweden started in 1863 when the Board for State Railways Operations was established which was basically a railway construction organisation. In 1888, it was reorganised into Statens Jarnvagar (SJ), i.e., the Swedish State Railways. Towards the end of the century a number of private investors considered it profitable to construct private railways due to the boom in the economy. By the 1930s, the length of private railways was more than 10,000 km out of about 17,000 km of the total length of railways. Most of the private railways were short distance local or regional railways. But soon the private companies faced tough competition from road which further eroded their already meagre profits. In 1935, the government decided to nationalise the private railways, a process which was completed by 1950.

By 1950, like most Railways of the world SJ had become a vertically integrated fully government-owned railway. SJ also owned and operated other rail-related businesses such as ferries, long distance bus services, freight forwarding agency etc.

The financial relationship between SJ and the government is best summarised as follows:

> SJ submitted an annual budget proposal to the Ministry of Transportation and Communications. This proposal included projections of revenue and operating expenses, as well as a submission for investment capital. SJ could not borrow from commercial lenders on the basis of its own credit worthiness, nor could it decide independently on its investment program. Rather, it was allocated investment resources at the discretion of the government.
>
> The difference between SJ's revenue and operating costs — its gross profit — was applied to two purposes. First, SJ maintained an account which represented its liability to the state (statskapital). This liability represented the sum of all investment resources previously allocated to SJ, net of capital repayments made during previous years. Gross profit was first applied to repay that portion of the statskapital account that was current and was due within the budget year.
>
> In calculating the current repayment portion of statskapital, two principles would apply: (1) different categories of investment would have specific economic depreciation terms over which initial capital allocations were to be repaid; (2) historical investment costs would be inflated to reflect the current cost of reinvestment. Gross profit was also to be used to pay a "Dividend" to

> the state. The size of the Dividend was based on a simple formula using the weighted average cost of government borrowing and the size of the outstanding statskapital account.[2]

SJ had little independence, be it in matters of policy, pricing, closure of loss making services etc. And like most railways it was highly influenced by politicians. It continued to suffer. Its financial position deteriorated day by day. This compelled the government to pass some Transport Policy Acts applicable not only to railways but to all modes of transport.

The reform of railways proceeded through a number of Transport Policy Acts of which the Acts of 1963, 1979, 1985 and the Act of 1988 are most important. The Act of 1988 created a new model in Railways structure which came to be known as the Swedish Model. It later formed the basis of various Directives issued by the European Union to its Member states on railway matters. The Acts mentioned above were followed by some other Acts which fine-tuned the structure, such as the Acts of 1998, 2001, 2004. But the basic structure was established by the Act of 1988.

The exercise of railway reform in Sweden is seen as an exercise in its deregulation.

> .... The chain of events should be seen as moves to protect an ailing industry and hold the cost of procuring unprofitable railway services as low as possible. The use of deregulation to strengthen the consumer perspective has at most been of secondary importance.[3]

These Transport Policy Acts aimed at providing financial relief to SJ in various ways to enable it to compete with road and to deregulate the rail transport market. It ultimately led to the unintended entry of private players into railways, but not in a big way. The state still continues to play a dominant role.

There were two main considerations which influenced the way the transport policy evolved: Most important was the paramount social welfare concern of the government. Normally, had the lines been based purely on commercial considerations, the loss making lines would have been closed. However, this

[2] Ron Kopicki and Louis S. Thompson, 'Best Methods of Railway Restructuring and Privatisation', World Bank.

[3] Jan-Eric Nilsson, 'Restructuring Swedish Railway System: The Unintentional Deregulation' Swedish National Road and Transport Research Institute, 2003.

was not acceptable, largely because of (1) social welfare considerations, (2) local political sentiments, (3) railways were seen as least polluting and (4) the need for balanced regional development. Therefore, it was felt that railways had to be kept alive even by subsidising. Further, it was felt that the main reason why railways were unable to meet competition from road was because of unfair burden of costs on railways. While railways had to bear the cost of infrastructure as well as rolling stock and operations, roadway did not bear the cost of infrastructure. Road hauliers paid only a nominal amount for the use of infrastructure. The amount paid by them was nowhere near the cost of constructing and maintaining the highways.

The realisation that the difference between the costs borne by railways and road hauliers was unfair led to the gradual implementation of the 'road model' in railways.

The Transport Policy Acts were applicable to all modes of transport. The main provisions of the Acts applicable to railways are given below.

The 1963 Transport Act separated the SJ network into two parts – the commercial network and the non-commercial network. The non-commercial network comprised local and regional lines which were not expected to make profit because of low volume of traffic and hence was subsidised by the government. The difference between Japanese Railways and the Swedish Railways need to be noted. In the case of JNR it was the local commuter traffic which was the source of profit while in the case of the Swedish Railways it was the source of loss. The primary reason for this difference was the difference in density of traffic. Sweden is quite spread out and sparsely populated. Japan is densely populated and the passenger traffic is concentrated along the line of rail providing readymade adequate passenger traffic.

In 1980, the non-commercial network was 50 per cent in length carrying only 10 per cent of traffic. The subsidy on the non-commercial lines amounted to 13 per cent of the total revenue of SJ.

The main provisions of the 1979 Act were as follows:

- Earlier the local counties were responsible for providing local public transport – which was mainly limited to buses and in a few cases tramways and local commuter trains. The 1979 Act created County Transport Authority (CPTA) in all the counties. And the CPTAs were made responsible for running local commuter trains as well. In turn, the CPTAS were to be compensated by the government in the form of annual subsidy for ten years. The subsidy was to be equal to the operating losses suffered by SJ on them prior to their being handed over to the CPTAs. CPTAs were also provided with rolling stock which they could rent out to private rail operators.

> This represented a first but important step in shifting the financial burden of non-commercial commuter rail services to the counties and away from the central government. It had the advantage of placing the financial responsibility for some money losing operations directly in the hands of those interests that had been most resistant to branch line abandonment.[4]

Compare this to the responsibility for suburban services including metro services in Kolkata borne by Indian Railways.

- The remaining part of the subsidised network was merged with commercial part of SJ on which it continued to receive government subsidy.

However, in spite of shifting the burden of non-profitable lines from SJ network to CPTAs and continued receipt of subsidy on the non-profitable services of the commercial network, the finances of SJ continued to suffer.

Therefore, further relief was provided by the Transport Act of 1985. According to this Act,

- The government accepted full responsibility for rail infrastructure as in the case of highways.
- SJ was instructed to separate the accounts for infrastructure from the rest of the accounts.
- Passenger and Freight Divisions were asked to pay internal fees to infrastructure accounts for the use of infrastructure. This was the first implementation of the 'road model' though only internally. Infrastructure and train operations were not separated into two different companies but only in respect of their accounts. Formal separation of infrastructure and operation followed later through the Act of 1988.

[4] Ron Kopicki and Louis S. Thompson, 'Best Methods of Railway Restructuring and Privatisation', World Bank.

- Earlier all investments were added to the capital of SJ as debt to be repaid to the government. And the historical cost was inflated to reflect present day reinvestment cost for the purpose of calculating the repayment amount. After the Act of 1985, only 80 per cent of the investment was to be added to debt and balance 20 per cent was treated as grant.
- After the 1985 Act the repayment was to be calculated on historical cost, not on inflated cost.
- But SJ was required to finance rolling stock procurement through market borrowing according to the limit set by the government every year. This was the first interaction of SJ with the financial market.
- SJ was asked to reorganise its subsidiaries which included – catering business, bus business, trucking, ferry, and freight forwarding. All these were reorganised into a holding company called Swedcarrier.
- The government wrote off SKr 1,877 million debt of SJ, which was the net book value of SJ assets on that day.
- SJ was asked to sell off its subsidiaries which did not complement with its core business of rail transport. This, however, did not prove very popular with SJ.

> In summary, the 1985 Railway Act meant: (1) infrastructure and operations were separately accounted for; (2) total investment allocations increased and the share of grants in these allocations grew; and (3) centralized control of SJ's management was further relaxed.[5]

The finances of SJ still continued to be poor. This led to the Transport Act of 1988 which was the most important of all Transport Policy Acts. It created what came to be popularly known as the Swedish model of railway structure.

> 'The 1988 reform was substantially an attempt to deal with a recurring financial deficit by way of organisational restructuring.'[6]

[5] Ron Kopicki and Louis S. Thompson, 'Best Methods of Railway Restructuring and Privatisation', World Bank.

[6] Jan-Eric Nilsson, 'Restructuring Swedish Railway System: The Unintentional Deregulation', Swedish National Road and Transport Research Institute, 2003.

It also changed the basic structure of the railway system.

> … the Transport Policy Act of 1988, with its ground-breaking split of railway infrastructure from operations, is commonly considered the starting point for transformation of the Swedish railway system – from a vertically and horizontally integrated monopoly to a market characterised by decentralisation and intra-modal competition.[7]

Four motives are generally given for the 1988 Act. One was to put railways on an equal footing with roadways by relieving railways from the responsibility for infrastructure. Secondly, since railways were considered uniquely safe and most environment-friendly means of transport, it was considered necessary to support the railways. Thirdly, to develop a mechanism for transferring the loss making local and regional lines to the responsibility of those who wanted to retain them on the principle of 'user pays'. And last, but most important was to arrest the deteriorating financial condition of railways.

The main provisions of the 1988 Act were:

- The Act of 1985 had required SJ only to maintain separate accounts for infrastructure and train operations, nothing beyond maintenance of separate accounts was required. The Act of 1988 formally divided SJ into two parts – infrastructure was separated from operations. Two independent companies were created – SJ (Statens Jarnavagar), the Swedish State Railways and Ban Verket (BV) National Rail Administration. Both the companies were fully state owned.
- BV was made responsible for infrastructure including track, electrical overhead equipment (OHE) and signalling. Investments in infrastructure as well as its cost of maintenance was to be financed by the government.
- SJ was responsible for owning rolling stock and running of trains. Initially, there was some controversy about the ownership of train control – both BV and SJ staking their claim. Ultimately the work of allotting track capacity and train control passed on to BV in July 1996.

---

[7] G. Alexandersson and S. Hulten, 'The Swedish Railway Deregulation Path', *Review of Network Economics*', Vol 7, 1 March 2008.

- SJ had monopoly over freight and long distance passenger business. It was mandated to run trains on commercial considerations and make profits. Loss making passenger services, if requisitioned by the government, were to be subsidised by the government.
- SJ was required to make payment to BV for use of infrastructure. However, as in the case of roadways the payment of access charges by SJ was not expected to cover the full cost of infrastructure. Access charges consisted of two parts – a fixed payment and a variable payment.
- Fixed payment was an annual fixed amount per vehicle owned by SJ. Variable charge was made up of five elements:

  (i) Different types of vehicles paid different charges per GTKM. This was to distinguish different wear and tear characteristics of different types of vehicles on the infrastructure.
  (ii) A charge for every kilometre of operation by electric trains to account for depreciation of the OHE.
  (iii) Accident charge per kilometre of train operation to cover cost of accidents such as – material damage, cost of hospitalisation, loss of production, insurance etc.
  (iv) Environment fee per litre of diesel used by diesel locomotives to reflect the cost of environment pollution.
  (v) Marshalling yard handling fee per handling in marshalling yards.

In 1999 the variable charges consisted of:

Trackage fee, passenger
Trackage fee, freight
Information fee, passenger
Accident charge, passenger
Accident charge, freight
Diesel charge
Shunting charge
Charge for using Oresund bridge, freight[8]

Although access charges were not expected to meet the full cost of infrastructure, still the realisation from the fees received by BV was not

[8] Jan-Eric Nilsson, 'Restructuring Swedish Railway System: The Unintentional Deregulation', Swedish National Road and Transport Research Institute, 2003.

adequate to meet even the maintenance cost of infrastructure. In 1990, the revenue realised as access charges from SJ was able to meet only 18 per cent of the maintenance cost of BV, leave aside any part of the capital cost.

As regards investments in infrastructure, the same road model was introduced. Investments were to be evaluated not in terms of financial returns but in terms of social cost-benefit, and the cost was to be borne by the government.

The reforms never aimed to introduce intra-modal, i.e., 'on-tack' competition in railways nor was entry of private sector in railways visualised. But entry of private train operators on the main lines was not barred either. The reforms were only aimed to strengthen the railways to meet inter-modal competition from road. However, the deregulation process created conditions in which the private sector did make its entry. This started with the CPTAs tendering for its rail services and awarding tenders on the basis of lowest cost irrespective of who the bidder was.

One of the most important factors inhibiting entry of private operators in capital-intensive rail business was the high cost of owning rolling stock, particularly due to uncertainty of winning the next tender for operating rights. This was resolved by transferring the ownership of rolling stocks for passenger service to CPTAs which could be taken by private operators on lease. This created level playing field and encouraged private operators to bid for train operations. Some CPTAs came together and formed a separate rolling stock leasing company called Transitio.

Similarly, many freight operating companies got formed in the early 1990s leading to complete deregulation of the freight services. And from 1996, any one 'fit, willing and able' could compete with SJ and operate freight trains. Thus, by 2002, SJ remained with exclusive operation rights in respect of long distance passenger services only.

In 2001, SJ was further split into several state-owned companies concentrating on different aspects of SJ's business – SJ AB for passenger services, SJ Green Cargo for freight services, AB Swedecarrier for real estate, heavy maintenance, EuroMaint for maintenance, TraffiCare for cleaning services and Unigrid for computer information systems. The last two were privatised in a few months. Thus, instead of one single company providing a gamut of train operations, there were now many different separate units doing it.

There are more than 20 train operating companies using BV. But most of them are very small, and in 2004 the state-owned SJ Ltd. which runs passenger trains had 88 per cent share of long distance and 54 per cent share of short distance passenger traffic and Green Cargo had 74 per cent market share of freight business.

Thus, the state with its ownership and maintenance of BV and a number of companies providing various types of services is still the biggest player in railways in Sweden.

But all the restructuring exercise has still (2003) not succeeded in reducing the financial burden of the government.

> ... the public sector's financial cost for support to the railway industry has increased substantially, from SEK 3 billion in 1987 to about SEK 9 billion in 1999 (mi-2001 price level). The bulk of the subsidies go to investment in new tracks....... In 1999 'Sweden's Railways would, therefore, not be able to pay their full costs if asked to do so'....... Sweden, today, subsidises its railway system heavily.[9]

The vertical separation of infrastructure and operations model of railway structure developed by Sweden triggered similar reforms in other countries of Europe.

Features of the Swedish Model

- The structure evolved over a period of time. Its features went on getting added one by one through many Transport Policy Acts.
- The structure of railways changed from a fully government-owned vertically integrated entity to a vertically separated entity where infrastructure is fully owned, financed and maintained by the government but train operation is partly in private hands.
- Train operators pay an access charge to infrastructure, which is too small to meet the cost of infrastructure. In fact, provision of infrastructure by the government is treated as a sort of social welfare act.
- The train operation by SJ is expected to be conducted on purely commercial consideration and earn profit. If a service which is not

[9] Jan-Eric Nilsson, 'Restructuring Swedish Railway System: The Unintentional Deregulation', Swedish National Road and Transport Research Institute, 2003.

expected to make profit, is requisitioned by the government, the losses are met by the government.

- The responsibility for local and regional train services was transferred to the counties. They could decide on running the service or closing it down depending the upon the demand of their citizens and the financial capability of the counties.
- In order to facilitate entry of private operators into railway business, the counties were provided with rolling stock which could be leased by the private operators.
- Many state-owned companies were created to provide different kinds of railway services to train operators. Some of these companies were later privatised.

The Swedish model has found favour with the European Union also which has issued many Directives to its Member states. Two of the Directives are important viz. Directive Number 91/440/EEC and Directive Number 2001/12/EC. These Directives required Member state to separate the accounts of infrastructure and operation (but not necessarily separate the two into two separate entities) and realise access charge for the use of infrastructure. The primary purpose of separating the two was to enable the creation of a European transport market so that trains of any Member state could run on the infrastructure of any Member state as in the case of road transport. No principle for fixing access charges were laid down. Each country could fix its own principle of charging. But no discrimination in levying of access charges was allowed irrespective of ownership of the train operating company.

As a theoretical railway structure, however, doubts about the wisdom and efficacy of separation of infrastructure and operation and entrusting them to separate organisations still persist.

7

British Railways

British Rail was privatised by the Conservative government of Prime Minister John Major in 1997. It was not the privatisation per se which was a failure but the structure that was created and the haste with which it was executed. There was nothing wrong on paper. But it was far from practicable. As is often said, the structure was created in a smoke-filled room by those who did not understand that rail industry is vastly different from other industries such as telecommunications, electricity, air ports and roads. There is, at present, a strong demand for re-nationalisation of railways in UK.

British Rail (BR) came into existence as a result of nationalisation of four large private railways by the Labour government of Prime Minister Atlee in 1948. BR was in bad shape right from the beginning due to long neglected infrastructure during the War years, falling traffic, defunct lines, stations and depots, overstaffing etc. As a consequence, it suffered from acute financial problems, so much so that for the first time BR failed to make even operating profits in 1955.

The government appointed the Stedeford Committee in 1961 to look into the affairs of British Rail. One of the Members of the Committee Dr Richard Beecham was appointed the Chairman of the British Railway Board (BRB) who later prepared a report titled 'The Reshaping of British Railways' in 1963. The main thrust of the report was on considerable trimming down of unprofitable lines and activities of BR. It recommended closing down of many railway lines, one-third of passenger services, 4,000 of 7,000 stations and retrenching large number of employees. The report was very unpopular among the public, labour unions and the railway management. It was called 'The Beecham Axe'. Predictably, it was not fully implemented. But quite a few of the recommendations were indeed implemented between 1963 and 1970. The network was curtailed from 29,117 in 1962 to 18,889 in 1970.

Whatever be the other merits or demerits of the Beecham Report, it is often credited with creating a broader understanding of the role of railways and introducing a more business-like approach to railway management. The railways in UK still bear the imprint of the Beecham Report.

But the finances of railways continued to deteriorate.

The British Railways followed a typical unified integrated structure then prevalent in railway industry throughout the world except for the Swedish Railways. The BR Board was headed by a Chairman, two Vice-Chairmen and Board Members for Finance, Personnel, Marketing (Passenger, Freight and Parcels), Engineering and Research and Operations and Productivity. The network was divided into five geographical regions headed by Regional Managers. The regions were divided into divisions and further sub-divided into Areas. Thus, BR followed a four-tier structure – the BR Board, regions, divisions and areas. And the Regional Managers 'had essentially full operating control over their area of the railway, but who had a cost, not a Net Revenue, objective.[1]

Another serious attempt at restructuring of BR was made by Sir Robert Reid in the 1980s when he was Chairman of the British Railway Board. He introduced the 'Business Sector' approach to railway management, each sector representing a particular type of railway business. The entire business of BR was classified into five Business Sectors – InterCity (long distance passenger traffic), Network South East (covering the commuter service around London), Provincial (covering largely unprofitable low density passenger services in the countryside), Freight and Parcels. Each sector was headed by a Sector Manager and was designated as a profit centre. This structure was based on the principle that different types of businesses required different types of customer focus and approach.

The Business Sector approach, however, did not prove successful.

> At the beginning of Sector Management, the Sectors mainly took responsibility for marketing and financial reporting, with almost all asset management and operating decisions remaining in the hands of the Regions. As management began to assign more importance to the sectors, more responsibility and authority was shifted to the sector managers, ultimately putting them in charge of rolling stock and train operations. The final phase of implementation

---

[1] Louis S. Thompson, 'Privatising British Railways: Are There Lessons for World Bank and its Borrowers', World Bank 2004.

creating fully-fledged business units and abolishing the Regions took place in the 1991–1993 period under the name of "Organizing for Quality." (OfQ).[2]

The Conservative government of Prime Minister Margaret Thatcher went about privatising most large British public sector undertakings with a missionary zeal – telecommunications, gas, electricity, air ports, air lines etc. The motto was 'The government has no business to be in business'. But the Thatcher government was extremely reluctant to privatise British Rail as it was considered a too complex and difficult task.

By the time the Conservative government of Prime Minister John Major came to power in 1992, there was not much left for it to privatise except the British Rail. John Major wanted to complete this remaining task before the next election in 1997 as he was unsure of coming to power again in 1997. At that time BR was being provided a subsidy of about 1.7 billion Pound Sterling per year. Thus, privatisation of BR was rooted as much in ideology as in the need of reducing the financial burden on the government. The process of BR privatisation was completed in break-neck hurry to beat the election schedule. It was started in 1993 and completed in 1997. Much of the problems faced later is ascribed to this sense of hurry.

In the meantime, a couple of developments had taken place in the railway sector in other parts of the world which affected the restructuring model in Britain.

The Japanese Railways had been privatised in 1987. JNR followed the structure of complete privatisation with vertical integration of functions and horizontal separation of area of operation in respect of passenger traffic and vertical separation of functions and horizontal integration of area of operation in respect of freight traffic.

The next major development was in Sweden in 1988 which innovated the concept of vertical separation, i.e., separation of infrastructure from train operation – each to be run by two separate government-owned companies.

The British government attempted everything at the same time. It separated infrastructure from train operations, i.e., vertical separation as in Sweden. Simultaneously, it also carved train operations into many companies, i.e., horizontal separation as in Japan. And it privatised all of them. All the three

---

[2] Louis S. Thompson, 'Privatising British Railways: Are There Lessons for World Bank and its Borrowers', World Bank 2004.

actions were carried out at the same time thus implementing vertical separation, horizontal separation and privatisation at one stroke. Such a massive all-round restructuring of railway business and that too in such a short time had not been attempted anywhere else in the world earlier, and has not been attempted since then.

After implementation of the privatisation scheme in 1997, many foreseeable and unforeseen problems kept cropping up. As a result, many patchwork solutions kept on being attempted. Many of them had to be redone. So many patches were introduced and so many structures changed one after the other that it is difficult to keep track and put together a coherent description of evolution of the events and the structures.

However, an attempt can be made to cull the main objectives of the scheme. They were to:

- Eliminate the need for government subsidy to railways which was to the tune of about 1.7 billion Pound Sterling per year.
- Bring in private investment both in infrastructure and in rolling stock.
- Create competition in all aspects of railway working in the belief that competition will improve performance, reduce cost, reduce fares and freights and thereby increase consumer satisfaction.

The main provisions of the original structure of 1997 are as follows:

- The physical infrastructure consisting of track, signalling, stations and depots was handed over to Railtrack who became the owner of infrastructure and was responsible for investment in and maintenance of the infrastructure. It was also responsible for allotting train paths and train control. Railtrack let out most of the 2509 stations to the concerned Train Operating Companies (TOCs) keeping only about a dozen of the most important ones under its own management. The track maintenance work was also contracted out to British Rail Infrastructure Services. Thus, most of the activities of Railtrack were contracted out. Consequently, Railtrack needed to keep only a handful of staff on its own rolls.
- 25 passenger train operating units, based on geographical area and service type, were created. Each passenger train operating unit was franchised out to a Train Operating Company (TOC) for 5 to 15 years. A TOC could bid and win more than one train operating units.

- The above franchising scheme in the case of passenger services was not followed for freight business. The freight business was sold outright to six Freight Operating Companies (FOCs).
- The rolling stock of BR was split into three Rolling Stock Companies (ROSCOs). The TOCs were expected to lease rolling stock for passenger train operation from the ROSCOs for bidding for a train path. In fact, the TOCs owned practically nothing except for the train crew. They hired rolling stock from ROSCOs and station facilities from Railtrack and other maintenance services from the service providing companies. Thus, their stake was very low.
- On the other hand, the FOCs were expected to have their own rolling stock.
- 19 companies were created to provide specific rail-related services which could be hired by the TOCs and the FOCs.
- The relationship between Railtrack, TOCs/FOCs, ROSCOs and OPRAF was governed by contracts leading to a plethora of two way and three way contracts resulting onto a complex web of contracts.
- Each TOC had monopoly of train operation on the lines it operated. Other operators could use the track section through an agreement with the TOC owning the section.
- The TOCs could operate any number of trains in the traffic operating units won by it.
- Government created two regulatory authorities viz. the Office of Passenger Rail Franchising (OPRAF) and Office of the Rail Regulator (ORR). The former was required to manage the franchising process for passenger train operators and the latter was charged with the responsibility of regulating passenger fares, protect other interests of the consumer, approve track access charges, monitor and regulate the working of ROSCOs and so on.
- The tendering for the train operating unit paths was organised by (OPRAF). This led to further three-way contracts between OPRAF, Railtrack and the TOC.
- The TOCs were expected to pay a track access charge to Railtrack which consisted of two parts – a fixed part and a variable part. In order to ensure a reasonably steady income to Railtrack the fixed part formed 91 per cent of the track access charge. The variable part varied with the number of trains pushed in by the TOC.

After privatisation was completed, BR was left with very little assets or activity and it was ultimately wound up and replaced with Strategic Rail Authority in 2001.

BR reform failed to meet its ambitious objectives in many ways.

- About 100 private companies had been created to which different parts and services of BR were sold off by the government. The relationship between the companies was governed by written contracts. It is easy to see how inconceivably difficult it would be to run a railway system in which the relationship among its various components is governed solely by a multitude of contracts. A railway system cannot be run by contracts alone as the primary concern of each component would be maximisation of its profits rather than running of trains. Soon it became too complex to manage and led to numerous disputes.

  In fact, interest of contracting parties were too conflicting to reconcile. A few examples would suffice.
  - Since variable part of the access charge was very low, it was in the interest of TOCs to push in as many trains as possible as long as it covered its marginal cost. On the other hand, since 91 per cent of the access charge was fixed, Railtrack had little interest in accepting additional trains. Running of more trains would have led to increased maintenance cost for which the compensation by way of additional variable charge was too meagre.
  - There was no incentive for Railtrack to improve its services or expand. This was in direct contrast to expectation of additional investment in infrastructure after privatisation.
  - TOCs expected traffic volumes to increase. Therefore, they had placed orders for better quality rolling stock which required improvements in infrastructure involving additional investment. Railtrack was in no mood to make those investments as it had no incentive to do so. This led to large number of undelivered rolling stock lying with the manufacturers. This affected manufacture of rolling stock.
  - There was also structural problem in the scheme. While Railtrack followed geographical structure, TOCs transcended geographical structure. Hence, the TOCs found it difficult to deal with many local geographical units of Railtrack.

- Railtrack was the butt of all dissatisfaction among the privatised railways companies be it the TOCs or the ROSCOs, and it was the first to fail. In fact, apart from laxity in management, there were some inbuilt factors in the privatisation scheme itself which contributed to the failure of Railtrack.
  - Before privatisation, the government had formed 13 geographically based infrastructure maintenance and track renewal companies within BR and sold them to private bidders. And the government had already entered into maintenance and track renewal contracts with them which were passed on to Railtrack after its formation. Since the contract had been awarded by the government and not by Railtrack, the latter found it difficult to manage the contractors.
  - As per contract, the contractor himself was required to decide what work was required and in which portion of the track. Naturally, the contractor selected only such items of work on such portion of the track which was easiest to handle and most lucrative, rather than that which was most required.

The track condition continued to deteriorate leading to a number of accidents besides extremely bad service quality. The Hatfield accident in 2000 was the last straw on the camel's back. The cause of accident was found to be rail fatigue. Railtrack immediately imposed 1200 emergency speed restrictions as it was not sure where else the rails were distressed. This led to vehement protests from the TOCs and the travelling public. The Hatfield accident also led to severe financial problems for Railtrack as it was required to carry out extensive repairs to the track.

Massive hue and cry by the public made political interference inevitable.

A year later Railtrack was put under railway administration by the British High Court and ultimately handed over to Network Rail, a newly formed company specifically for this purpose. In 2004, Network Rail took over the maintenance of infrastructure, leaving the work of track renewal to private contractors.

- One of the most important considerations in the privatisation of BR was to introduce all round competition. What eventually happened was far different. Infrastructure was handed over to only one company Railtrack. Actually, this was inevitable. Rail infrastructure, in fact, is a natural monopoly due to its excessively capital-intensive nature and practically nil opportunity of its alternative use – the non-contestability theory. It is difficult to visualise a parallel competing line next to an existing line except partly in Japan and in USA.

- Even in respect of train operating companies, competition got limited only to winning the tender. Once a traffic operating unit was franchised to a TOC, on-track competition got eliminated. The TOCs effectively became a monopoly, though a private monopoly. A private monopoly is far worse than a government monopoly. In many cases, at the time of next bidding or through the process of take-overs, foreign railways or companies which were state owned, became the TOCs. Some such examples are given in Table 7.1.[3]

Table 7.1: Ownership of privatised British Railways 2012

British Rail	*Franchise*	*Foreign Owners*
InterCity Cross Country	Cross Country Trains	Deutsche Bahn
Network SouthEast Chiltern	Chiltern Railway	Deutsche Bahn
Merseyrail part of Regional Railways	Merseyrail	Nederlandse Spoorwegen
Regional Railways	Arriva Trains Wales	Deutsche Bahn
Regional Railways	Northern Rail	Nederlandse Spoorwegen
InterCity East Coast	Grand Central	Deutsche Bahn
InterCity Anglia	Greater Anglia	Nederlandse Spoorwegen
Network SouthEast	London Overground Rail Operations	50% owned by Deutsche Bahn and 50% by MTR
Network South East and Regional Railways	London Midland	35% owned by SNCF
Network SouthEast	Southern Trains	35% owned by SNCF
Network SouthEast	Southeastern Railway	35% owned by SNCF

Source: Neil Clarke, Neil Clarke, 'The public wants railway nationalised – what are we waiting for?, The Guardian, 4 October 2012.

[3] Neil Clarke, 'The public wants railway nationalised – what are we waiting for?', *The Guardian*, 4 October 2012.

- The purpose of splitting BR rolling stock into three ROSCOs was to encourage competition amongst them so that they keep supplying improved rolling stock to the TOCs at the lowest cost. This also did not happen. The requirement of rolling stock of different TOCs was so different that they got hooked on to one or other of the ROSCOs who took advantage of this in their pricing. Further, the quality of stock also did not improve as there was no incentive for the ROSCOs to do so. In fact, it is said that the only people to benefit from BR privatisations were the owners of ROSCOs who made huge profits. Most of the owners of the ROSCOs were ex-employees of BR who had formed separate companies for this purpose.
- Two other integral elements of the ROSCO scheme viz. that the ROSCOs will supply rolling stock to TOCs only and secondly that no one else other than ROSCOs will own rolling stock also did not hold. The ROSCOs started supplying stock to FOCs also and with passage of time some TOCs and Network Rail started purchasing their own rolling stock directly from manufacturers instead of leasing them from the ROSCOs.
- Financially also the privatisation scheme was not a success. Before privatisation, in 1994 the government subsidy to BR was 1.627 billion Pound Sterling (2.168 Pound Sterling in terms of 2005 prices) while it was 4.593 billion Pound Sterling in 2005.[4]

It is true that there were a lot of physical improvements shortly after privatisation – punctuality improved, number of trains increased, volume of traffic increased, quality of on-board service improved, quality of passenger coaches improved. But these were short lived. And there is still a debate whether the volume of traffic increased because of privatisation or because of boost in the British economy. In the meantime, passenger fares skyrocketed.

At present, there is considerable doubt even among the leaders of the Conservative Party, who had introduced the BR privatisation scheme, about its success. Several options for the future are being discussed including shift to a system where regional operators own the track and trains for their regions, i.e., region-wise vertical integration followed by Japan. In 2012, Labour

[4] Neil Clarke, 'The public wants railway nationalised – what are we waiting for?', *The Guardian*, 4 October 2012.

leader Ed Miliband also hesitantly suggested that the Party may put a promise to renationalise the Railways in their 2015 general election manifesto.

> "As an interesting postscript to the privatisation, in July 2006 the Conservative Party's shadow transport spokesman, Chris Grayling, admitted that the 1996 split of the rail industry into track and train components was a mistake which had increased costs.
>
> 'We think, with hindsight, that the complete separation of track and train into separate businesses at the time of privatisation was not right for our Railways. We think that the separation has helped push up the cost of running the Railways—and hence fares—and is now slowing decisions about capacity improvements. Too many people and organisations are now involved in getting things done—so nothing happens. As a result, the industry lacks clarity about who is in charge and accountable for decisions." [5]

Another observation reflects the mood of the nation.

> "The problem seems to be that despite the financial crash of 2008, Britain's political elite are still in thrall to neoliberal dogma. This dogma holds that nationalised industries are inherently "inefficient" and that "private sector solutions" are always best. But this flies in the face of the evidence of the past 33 years. No one who travels regularly on the eminently affordable, reliable and comfortable state-operated Railways of, say, Germany and France could say – hand on heart – that they are less efficient than Britain's overcrowded and hideously expensive privatised trains. It may not be fashionable in elite circles to say it but British Rail did a much better job – and with much less public money – than its privately run successors.[6]

The last word on reform of British rail is yet to be heard.

---

[5] Neil Clarke, 'The public wants railway nationalised – what are we waiting for?', *The Guardian*, 4 October 2012.

[6] Ibid.

8

Some Other Railways

This chapter presents a very brief survey of the reforms in Russian Railways, German Railways and Chinese Railways.

Russian Railways

The first railways in Russia were built in 1839. Though most of them were privately owned and operated, they were heavily supported and financed by the government. With the impending WW 1 the Tsarist government started nationalising many private railways, a process which was completed by the communist government. During the pre-reform era the railway was divided into 17 regional railways closely controlled by the central government including pooling and redistribution of revenues. It was controlled by the Ministry of Means of Communications. After the introduction of reforms, the regional railways became branch offices of the Russian Railways.

Russian Railways is a government-owned vertically integrated railway. With 85,000 km of track it is one of the largest rail networks in the world. It holds more than 1 million freight cars, 20,200 locomotives and has more than 1.2 million employees. Russian Railways consist of 987 enterprises and 185 subsidiaries. It is predominantly a freight-oriented railway carrying more than 1.3 billion tons of traffic. Oil, cement, iron ore and container services are the main items of freight. It carries about 80 per cent of freight traffic and 40 per cent of passenger traffic of the country. There is heavy element of cross-subsidisation. Freight revenue subsidises passenger traffic and oil, cement, iron ore etc. subsidise coal. The average lead of freight traffic varies from 1500 to 1900 km.

In 2001, the Russian government embarked upon the plan to reform its railways through Decree No. 384 called 'A Program for Structural Reform of Railway Transport'. It aimed at (1) increased reliability, safety, and quality of railway transport; (2) cutting overall transport costs in the economy; and (3) meeting the increasing demand for transportation. A number of reform principles were declared to achieve stated goals, such as

- Encouraging on-track competition
- Provision of non-discriminatory access to infrastructure
- Developing tariff policy to eliminate cross-subsidies
- Ensuring the state control over infrastructure of federal railways'[1]

The Decree of 2001 set out three distinct stages of reform to be accomplished within a period of ten years from 2001.

Phase 1 (2001–03)

- Formal creation of Joint Stock Company Russian Railways RZhD which was to remain government owned.
- Separation of RZhD and its business operations from the regulatory and policy making functions of the government.
- Divestment of non-core, non-commercial assets and activities of RZhD such as hospitals, hotels and schools.

Phase 2 (2003–05)

- Creation of RZhD subsidiaries as 'daughter companies' for freight, long distance passenger services, commuter services, construction, repair and infrastructure.
- Implementation of non-discriminatory infrastructure access for independent train operators.
- Sale of some RZhD rolling stock and locomotives to those operators.
- Implementation of transparent structure for government subsidies for passenger operation, to replace the historic cross-subsidisation from freight.

---

[1] Andrei Dementiev, 'Vertical Divestiture as a Competitive Strategy: The Case of Russian Railway Reform', 4th Annual Conference on' Railroad Industry Structure, Competition and Investment' Universidad Carlos III de Madrid, Spain, October, 2006.

Phase 3 (2006–10)

- Partial or complete privatisation of non-infrastructure subsidiary companies.
- Creation of competitive market for freight and possibly long distance passenger operation.

In accordance with the above scheme,

- The Ministry of Railways was renamed the Federal Rail Transport Agency (FTRA) with regulatory functions and responsibility for implementing the reform programme as well as licensing of federal railway activities.
- The fully government-owned Joint Stock Company Russian Railway was created as the corporate successor to the erstwhile Ministry of Railways.
- A number of government-owned subsidiaries were created. Important subsidiaries are:
    - JSC Transcontainer - for container services
    - JSC Refservices - for perishables
    - JSC Freight One - freight services
    - JSC Roszheldorproekt - design work
    - JSC Roszheldorstroy - construction of infrastructure
    - JSC Elteza - Manufacture and maintenance of rail control equipment
- In addition to the above joint stock companies, there are over a hundred private companies specialising in freight transportation, manufacture and repair of track equipment, manufacture and repair of rolling stock etc.

While still in the third Phase of the 2001 Program, the government issued another Order No. 877 in 2008 called 'The Strategy for Railway Development in the Russian Federation to 2030' which lays down plan for equipment modernisation and network expansion.

By 2011, the JSC Russian Railways, though government owned, was fully separated from the government and has succeeded in even raising capital from the market. The government plans to offer the shares of the company to private investors. However, at present there is divergence of opinion among the authorities both in the extent of devolution, varying from 5 per cent to 25 per cent, and the manner of devolution, from straightaway public offering or initially through private placement with banks. This divergence of opinion is largely because of the assessment that in a few years' time the market value of the shares will go up. But there is no in-principle difference on the fact that the shares of the company need to be devolved. The main reason forcing devolution of the shares is the massive need to modernise the locomotive stock and expansion of the network and the inability of the government to finance such a huge investment, EURO 10 billion for locos alone.

Most of the non-core activities have been either spun off or given up.

Private companies own about a third of rolling stock, except for locomotives. And the two thirds of the rolling stock which remain in the public sector are owned by Freight One and Freight Two which are government companies. But the government has embarked on sale of the wagon fleet in a big way. In 2011, RZhD sold government owned First Cargo Company which owned more than 190,000 wagons. Consequently, the share of private wagon fleet increased from 22 per cent in 2001 to 73 per cent in 2011. Liberalisation of the locomotive fleet is also expected by analysts in a few years' time.

Infrastructure and locomotives continue to be owned by the government. Private freight train operators can on attach their trains behind the government owned locomotives to be hauled on government-owned infrastructure.

The government mandated cross-subsidisation still remains. And none of the important subsidiaries have been privatised.

On-track competition in transportation of freight has not materialised in any significant way, one of the main reasons being that it has not been possible to develop proper tariff for infrastructure services by the government-owned infrastructure company.

A few elements of the reform scheme are noticeable –

- Infrastructure and operations are separated.
- Infrastructure would continue to be owned and managed by the government at least for the foreseeable future.
- As everywhere else, determination of satisfactory basis for access charge is a problem.
- Other items of rolling stock are being off loaded to finance locomotive modernisation and expansion of network.

German Railways

Prior to the unification of the two Germanys in 1991, there were two government owned railways – Deutsche Bundesbahn DB (West Germany) and Deutsche Reichbahn DR (East Germany). The railway reform Bill was passed in 1993 merging the two railways to create the German Railway Corporation DB AG as a joint stock company with 100 per cent shares owned by the government.

The main reasons for reform were – increasing competition from road, bureaucratic structure, too much government interference and mounting financial losses. The total debt of both DB and DR was to the tune of DM 70 billion. Two other factors played important roles in the decision to reform – added financial burden on DB to bridge the huge technical gap between DB and DR and secondly modernisation in order to take advantage of the central location of German Railways in the transport market of Europe which was undergoing economic revival.

Two developments influenced the structure which was finally created – the structures created in Japan and Sweden where reforms had already taken place and the issue of Directive EC/91/440 by the European Union which required all Member states to separate the accounts of the rail infrastructure and operation. The aim of the EU Directive was to enable movement of trains of other Member states or private railway companies on infrastructure owned by other Member states in order to create a large transport market and have seamless movement of all forms of transport over it. However, the Directive did not mandate any state to necessarily permit movement of the trains of other Member states or private companies on their system. It was to be purely voluntary depending upon mutual Agreement.

The main elements of the reform of 1993 were as follows:

- DBAG was divided into three Divisions – Track, Passenger transport and Freight transport, though still government owned.
- Two public-interest institutions were created. One to execute such functions which were considered to be legitimately the function of the state such as supervising, licensing and preparation of investment plans. The other institution was to absorb the long-term liabilities of DB and DR as well as surplus staff. It would also sell the surplus land belonging to DB and DR in order to clear the debt. The second institution had similar function as the Japanese National Railway Settlement Corporation.
- It was planned that after 3 years the three Divisions would be separated into three independent entities with DBAG as the holding company.

- And after 8 years the holding company will also be broken up. This would lead to complete separation of infrastructure and train operations.
- The Federal government would extend interest free loan to the Track company to finance the construction and replacement of lines according to the overall network plan of the government. In addition, the regional governments and even private parties could finance construction and maintenance of railway lines. The DBAG was also free to raise resources from the market to finance any construction if it found it financially advisable to do so.
- In all cases the Track company would bear the cost of maintaining and operating the lines.
- The Track company would pay to the Federal government an annual depreciation which in a way amounted to the Track company repaying the loan from the Federal government. This rule, however, concerned only the lines which were commercially viable. In case of lines which were not commercially profitable, the depreciation would be reduced or completely eliminated.
- In case of funds raised by the Track company itself from the market for financing the construction of lines, it would pay both depreciation and interest on those funds to the creditors.
- The responsibility for providing suburban passenger services was transferred to the regional governments or communities on the principle that those who want the services should pay for them on the principal of 'user pays'. However, the Constitution entitles the regional governments and communities to receive a part of the fuel tax to provide suburban passenger rail transport. Under this arrangement the rail company is commercially protected.
- The train operator will pay an access charge to the Track company. Thus, DBAG which is a government company as well as third party train operator, pays access charges for use of infrastructure to Track which also is a government company. However, as in all such cases, no satisfactory algorithm for charging access fee has yet been devised. But whatever the algorithm, no discrimination is allowed between one operator and another operator. Broadly the charge is based on time slot desired, weight of train, distance covered on different line sectors etc.

After reforms the volume of traffic has increased and debt has been coming down. At present the network is of 33,600 km. having 5,700 stations. DBAG runs 26000 passenger trains carrying 2.7 billion passenger and 412 million tons of traffic per year.

Chinese Railways

China is the latest entrant to railway reform although manufacturing activities and some other activities had been shed off quite some time back.

Chinese Railways (CR) is the largest rail network in the world, next only to USA. Till recently it was a monolithic organisation under the Ministry of Railways responsible for all aspects of work including policy, operation and regulation. Before 1981, it had no financial responsibility. All earnings were deposited with the government and all expenses were met by the government. Investment and prices were controlled by the government. Profit or loss was the responsibility of the government. Small changes were made between 1981–85.

In 1986, CR finances were separated from the government finances and a contract system called the Economic Contract Responsibility System (ECRS) between the government and the Ministry of Railways was introduced in which revenue, expenditure and capital investment was managed and controlled by the MOR on contract basis. The government phased out its direct financing of investments. A system of loan to the MOR was introduced.

The next evolutionary stage was emergence of Joint Ventures between the MOR and provincial governments or other entities who were interested in having new lines. The JVs were responsible for the construction and operation of the new lines. This ended the regime of central government ownership and responsibility of operation on the entire network. Quite a few such branch lines came up. The main national network, however, remained with the government.

A 'Policies for Encouraging non-central Government Funds to Build and Operate Railways'was issued in 1992.

'Its main concerns were

- Clarification of the relationship between investment, ownership and rewards.
- Establishing a co-operative venture and running railways as a business.
- Clearly defining the responsibilities, rewards and risks between partners.

- Relaxing tariff control.
- Reducing tax level.
- Availability of loan on favourable terms.
- A certain degree of open access.
- Permitting railway diversification, such as commercial use of land, tourism etc.'[2]

22 JVs got established by 1995 with total length of 7933 km. Stocks were also sold off for the purpose of raising funds. For example 30 per cent of shares of Guang-Shen Railway were sold off in Hong Kong Stock Exchange for HK$ 5 billion in 1996.

The next stage in evolution was in the form of disbanding the Ministry of Railways. In March 2013 the Ministry of Railways was dissolved and its functions split into three parts –

- Railway policy and planning was entrusted to the Ministry of Communications (MOC)
- Administrative function was assigned to State Railway Administration (SRA)
- Operation and commercial activities were assigned to Chinese Railway Corporation (CRC)

CRC will report directly to the central government i.e. to the State Council. It will be responsible for the business activity of railways. It will also prepare the railway construction plan and execute it after the approval of the government. CRC will be regulated by MOC and SRA, though the nature and extent of control to be exercised by the two agencies is not yet quite clear.

SRA will be responsible for framing technical standards, overseeing railway safety and service quality and ensure that railway projects are implemented according to the required standards. SRA also will report to MOC.

> Incorporation of the railway sector into MOC is part of the reform scheme aimed at building up a comprehensive national transport system.
>
> ... The Government is studying the introduction of subsidy socially necessary rail services. Losses incurred for the carriage of students, disabled

[2] Jian Wong Wu and Chris Nash 'Railway Reform in China', Institute of Transport Studies, University of Leeds, Working Paper 524, 1998.

military personnel and agricultural products at very low rates and operation on Quinghai-Tibet and Southern Xinjiang lines are likely to be compensated for by the state.[3]

One problem is the mammoth debt on CRC arising almost entirely on account of the huge expansion of the railway network and implementation of superior technology. In fact, China is now regarded as a leader in railway technology. The debt amounts to about $428 billion. Various proposals are being considered. One of the proposals which is likely to be accepted by the Government is to relieve CRC of past debts. CRC will be responsible only for future debts.

Thus China is well on the path of reforming its railway system. Three things need to be noted – the separation of policy making, execution and regulatory functions; compensation for Public Service Obligations and that even in a communist regime efforts are being made to run railways as commercial concerns.

[3] Jian Wong Wu and Chris Nash 'Railway Reform in China', Institute of Transport Studies, University of Leeds, Working Paper 524, 1998.

Part 3

Reforming Indian Railways

9

What Others Did

The survey of railway reforms in some countries in Part 2 reveals some interesting features. The basic problems forcing governments to reform their railways were more or less the same in all the railways and the solutions aimed at were also more or less the same. But they differed widely in the method adopted to reach those solutions. They created very different structures. This was because of different local compulsions – such as the traffic-mix, concentration or dispersal of traffic, financial condition of the government, political and social goals to be achieved, market conditions etc. There are lessons to be learnt. But Indian Railways need not, in fact cannot, emulate their methods or structures completely. It must formulate its own strategy to suit its entirely different local conditions and compulsions.

Reasons for reform

All the railways suffered from similar afflictions.

- At the time of reform all railways were owned and controlled by respective governments. The railways had little leeway in framing policies, tariffs, investments, appointment to top management positions and so on.
- There was too much political interference in railways.
- The railways were in huge financial debt. Most of them were not able to meet even their operating expenses.
- The governments subsidised railways, causing immense pressure on government finances.
- The railways had huge surplus staff and powerful trade unions.
- They were facing tough competition from other modes of transport particularly road and in some cases by air and coastal shipping.
- Railway management lacked clear focus due to mix-up between Public Service Obligations and the need to remain afloat.

- Railway managements had become complacent due to continued dependence on government financial support.
- Railway management lacked the incentive to perform.
- The railways had become production oriented and unmindful of the need to make profit.

In all cases, the reforms were triggered by acute financial condition of the railways and the inability and /or reluctance of the governments to continue to shoulder the burden of railways due to their own precarious financial situation.

Aims of reform

There were basically three aims which the governments sought to achieve. They tried to create railways which could:

- be financially self-sufficient
- successfully face competition from other modes of transport
- provide adequate and quality service

They tried to achieve them in various ways. But the methods adopted by them had some common features.

Common features of reform

- All reforms were undertaken at the initiative of the government.
- It was explicitly accepted that railways were in fact a commercial undertaking like any other commercial venture.
- Realising that government bureaucratic structure was totally unsuitable for a commercial entity like railways, the governments put as much distance as possible between the government and railways. The methods devised fall into a wide spectrum. Japan and Britain went to the extent of privatisation. The others created different government-owned companies for different railway activities and provided them with almost as much flexibility as normally available to a private company.
- The government relieved railways of their debt and surplus staff. This played a major role in the rejuvenation of the railways.
- The governments continued to provide subsidy to railways in different forms – meeting cost of infrastructure construction and maintenance, advancing interest free loan for the construction of infrastructure,

paying for non-remunerative services etc. The last named took care of Public Service Obligation of the government without burdening the railways or compromising on their commercial focus.

- Railway management was given clear mandate to run railways on commercial lines and be financially self-sufficient.
- In some cases financial incentives for the management was also introduced.

Though the broad features of the reform were the same, the structures created by the railways varied widely as described in Part 2.

The causes leading to reform described above bear uncanny resemblance with the Indian conditions except in one respect. Indian Railways is still able to make some profit after meeting huge cost of Public Service Obligations and paying Dividend to the government. However, making small profit and payment of Dividend (deferred in many years) by Indian Railways can in no way be taken as an indication of healthy finances. In fact, as shown in Chapter 3, even the so-called profit could well amount to an artificially propped up profit by denying adequate appropriation to the Depreciation Reserve Fund. The profitability or otherwise can become clear only after its accounts are recast on commercial principles.

No one disputes that Indian Railways is facing an abyss and is in urgent need of reform. The question which has remained unsettled is: What form should it take?

Many committees in the past have dealt with this issue, but not in much detail, perhaps because it did not form a major part of their task except for the Railway Reforms Committee (1984). The Rakesh Mohan Committee (2001) dealt with the subject in greater detail. But they also dealt with it in a limited manner. They basically recommended (i) separation of Indian Railway's function into policy, execution and regulation and assigning the three functions to three different bodies (ii) corporatisation (iii) compensating IR for the cost of Public Service Obligations and iv) off-loading non-core activities. All these recommendations are very valid but not adequate.

Desirable features for Indian Railways

The governments which attempted reform in their railways created structures which were drastically different from the existing structures. They were nothing less than revolutionary.

It is contended that the existing structure on Indian Railways is basically sound. However, it is not working as well as it can. Therefore, the drastic methods adopted by other countries are neither necessary nor practicable in the case of Indian Railways. Similar results can be achieved by creating appropriate institutional framework and mechanisms more or less within the existing structure. Some tweaking may, of course, be unavoidable.

There are basically two problems relating to Indian Railways – excessive external interference and total absence of commercial orientation. The measures proposed in this book attempt to deal with these two issues. The emphasis is on creation of appropriate institutions. It is argued that the success of any measures to improve Indian Railways is highly doubtful in the absence of proper institutional framework. And once these mechanisms are created, improvements in railways will logically follow in a self-generating manner.

In the year 2009, Indian Railways published its 'Vision 2020' outlining its policies, aims and objectives for the coming decade. It did recognise the problems relating to the organisational structure of Indian Railways and said that

> As the competition from road and the aviation sectors hots up and expectations of customers rise, an organisation steeped in a departmental and differentiated culture would prove increasingly rigid and incapable of analysing and responding to the challenges. One possible approach to address this issue could be to reconfigure the organisation by separating infrastructure from operation and reorganise on business lines i.e. passenger, freight and parcel and other auxiliary services so that each could be managed and measured on a profit-centre basis. Areas other than the core operations, where appropriate, could be corporatised to impart business focus and managerial autonomy for such tasks.[1]

The Vision Statement talks of two important components of restructuring both to be undertaken together viz. separation of infrastructure and train operation, i.e., the Swedish model and separation of passenger, freight, parcel etc into separate profit centres, i.e., the British Sectoral model. It is important to deal with them before proceeding further.

Though separation of infrastructure and train operations has been adopted by quite a few countries, it has not yet been conclusively proved that it is a better model. This is largely because of two factors.

---

[1] Indian Railways, Vision 2020.

- Foremost is the difficulty in developing a satisfactory methodology to determine track access charges. Many theoretical constructs and econometric models have been developed without much satisfactory results. The access charges formulae used by different countries is shrouded in mystery. A high degree of subjectivity and arbitrariness still exists. In Sweden, for example, the access charges are not expected to meet even the maintenance cost of infrastructure. The balance unmet cost is the responsibility of the government. Even the European Union which prescribed separation of the accounts of infrastructure and operation and payment of access charges by the latter to infrastructure refrained from suggesting any formulae for determining the charges.
- Further, unless the infrastructure is wholly the responsibility of the government as in Sweden and funds are not a problem, it is impossible to ensure that the owner of the infrastructure will maintain or upgrade the infrastructure according to the needs of traffic and rolling stock unless it is profitable to him. This was in ample evidence in British Rail where the interest of the two were in direct conflict with each other, leading to all sorts of problems.

The reason why EU and Sweden introduced separation of infrastructure and train operation also needs to be kept in mind. In Sweden the main reason was to introduce the 'road model' with a view to relieve railways of the cost of infrastructure in order to promote fair inter-modal competition between road and rail.

EU recommended separation of accounts only, not separation of the two as separate entities, for infrastructure and train operation (and consequently having an access charge regime), for a different reason. It wanted to create a large unified rail transport market covering all its Member countries just as in case of road vehicles which was already in existence. The biggest impediment in doing so was the problem in charging of proper access fee. Unless the accounts for infrastructure were separated from that of train operations it was not possible to determine an access fee. But it refrained from prescribing any charging formulae because of the complexity involved. The access charge methodology was left to the discretion of individual railways. It only prescribed that there must not be any discrimination between one train operator and the other irrespective of the owner of the operator. For example, a country/railway could not have one methodology for charging its own train operator and another methodology for charging access fee from some other train operator.

According to Louis Thompson, one of the foremost railway experts with the World Bank,

> Vertical separation can be made to work, and is not unsafe: it is, however, expensive and poses difficulty in reconciling the interests of all parties. It remains to be seen whether the benefits are worth the costs. ... Bank clients who are not compelled to adopt the vertically separated approach should consider other options .... There was, and is, legitimate concern over the implication for efficiency and safety of the separation of infrastructure ownership and control from passenger and freight operations on the infrastructure.
>
> The infrastructure separation approach had appeal because of the possibility that competition on the network could be introduced while, at the same time, preserving the economies of scale in network planning and management: problems of coordination and interactions among all the pieces were not considered to be insurmountable. Since the Government's privatization of the electricity and telecom industries, along with airports and bus franchises, had generally adopted the model of a regulated infrastructure provider serving separated (sometimes competitive) operators, the argument to do the same for BR seems to have prevailed, **without a full realization of the ways in which rail differs from the other network industries.**[2] (emphasis mine)

Sometimes analogy is drawn with airports, seaports, telecommunications etc. It is argued that if airports and airlines can be two different entities, why not rail infrastructure and train operator. Suffice it to reiterate the above-mentioned opinion of one of the foremost railway experts that '**rail differs from the other network industries**'.

Thus, separation of infrastructure and train operations cannot be taken as a standard restructuring option.

As regards the business sector approach, it was first tried out by British Rail with less than encouraging results. For any business sector to be treated as a profit centre, the first requirement would be to separate the revenues and costs

[2] Louis S. Thompson, 'Privatising British Railways: Are There Lessons for World Bank and its Borrowers', World Bank 2004.

of each profit centre. While this would not pose much problem for revenue separation, it would be virtually impossible in respect of costs unless a purely arbitrary method is adopted, without much rationale for the method adopted. As is well known, more than seventy per cent of railway costs, particularly infrastructure costs, are joint costs and no satisfactory method has yet been devised for apportioning them among various services or costing units. How does one segregate the cost of track maintenance or station operations or the salaries of indirect staff among passenger, freight and parcel services? Indian Railways do have a Traffic Costing methodology, devised in the mid-1960s, which makes such segregations and produces Traffic Costing data every year. But the method followed is too gross and highly disputed. Indian Railways has not yet been able to revise the methodology in spite of pious wishes often expressed to do so.

In the Rakesh Mohan Committee Report a debate seems to have ensued between what were called the 'repairists' and the 'reinventionists'. The former favouring repair of the existing systems and the latter 'reinventing' the IR system and the majority seemed to tilt towards 'reinvention'. Perhaps, the'repairists' should have had the day. The suggestions contained in this book can be classified only as 'repairist'. Indian Railways is too vast and complex to be experimented with. Quite satisfactory results can be obtained even by less obtrusive measures.

So, how should one approach reform of Indian Railways? The operative words are 'cautiously but definitely'. The reform measures:

- Should be simple such that its rationale and structure should be clear down the line of the organisation. Only then will its acceptability and implementation be high. One of the main reasons for the failure of the British Rail reform was the complex structure created for it. Though there was nothing wrong on paper, it was far from implementable. Though the Swedish and the Japanese models were very different from the existing models, they were not overly complex. That is why they were more successful.
- In the Indian context the reforms should not be drastically different from the current structure and practices. Again a question of acceptability and implementability.
- It should be least intrusive and obtrusive.
- It should not be hurried but paced over a period of time. A planned stage-wise implementation process will be the key to success.

- Reform measures should be holistic, covering both external and internal factors, physical institutions and mechanisms as well as soft issues such as mindset and aptitudes. Piecemeal approach is unlikely to yield satisfactory results.
- Professionalisation at all levels has to be the key.
- In a competitive environment the structure must give preference to merit over seniority.

The reforms measures proposed in this book try to follow the above precepts as closely as possible.

Commercialisation of Indian railways is the central theme of this book. And all measures suggested herein are designed with this single goal in mind. The fact that railways is a purely commercial venture like any other industry, would be most difficult to accept not only by other than railwaymen but even by railwaymen, who have been long steeped in the very convenient characterisation of Indian Railways as a 'commercial cum public utility service'.

10

Commercialising Indian Railways

Why commercialise?

No other factor has caused greater harm to Indian Railways, its users and the Indian economy than its characterisation as a 'commercial cum public utility service'.

Therefore, this is the first question which must be tackled in the context of reforms in Indian Railways. What do we mean by commercialisation of Indian Railways and why at all should it be commercialised? Would the interest of the user and the economy be best served by such a change of its character?

In common parlance the word 'commercialisation' has come to acquire a rather vulgar connotation. It implies debasing something for the purpose of single-minded pursuit of profit or exploitation in complete disregard of all other considerations; commercialisation of religion, for example. In this sense, commercialisation of anything can hardly be supported. Even in the commercial world one needs to draw a distinction between 'profiteering' and earning profit.

While profiteering is an offensive word, profit is not. Profit is the *sine qua non* of all economic activity. It is the sole justification for economic activity. It acts as the most powerful rationale of and incentive for any economic activity. Apart from providing succour to those who undertake the activity and much needed finance to expand and grow, it is also the single most representative measure of efficiency, economy, customer focus and what have you. Therefore, the aim of all commercial entities is to maximise profit, albeit within the boundaries of law and morality.

In a competitive environment the market acts as the regulator of exploitative profit. In a non-competitive or imperfectly competitive environment, such as Indian Railways, some statutory regulation becomes necessary.

The characterisation of Indian Railways as a 'commercial cum public utility service' is not quite peculiar to Indian Railways. All railways of the world were similarly characterised till the late eighties, which led the railways to much grief. Railways came to be regarded as a sunset industry.

Why was this so?

The worst effect of characterising railways as a 'commercial cum public utility service' is not knowing where the 'public utility 'role ends and where the 'commercial entity' role begins. Such a label for railways was convenient both to politicians and to railwaymen, though for entirely different reasons. But as described earlier by the late 1980s, forced by disastrous financial consequences inherent in such a belief, many governments including those in communist countries such as Russia and China gradually realised this error of perception. Therefore, in all countries the essence of reform lay in accepting that like other economic activities, railways also is a purely commercial activity and it must be run as such. Once this was accepted other things were fairly easy. All reform measures were built around this central tenet.

The Acworth Committee (1921) too characterised Indian Railways as a purely commercial undertaking. But somewhere down the line this was given a go by and IR came to be characterised as a 'commercial cum public utility service'. When and how this happened is not quite clear. But it has turned out to be most confusing and disastrous to say the least. An organisation cannot be both a commercial venture and a public utility service at the same time. Trying to reconcile two irreconcilable objectives. How can it take up financially unviable activity, provide free or concessional service and simultaneously make its ends meet is not quite clear. Such a mandate also blurs organisational goals and allows inefficiencies to be swept under the carpet under the guise of public utility service.

Unless the commercial character of Indian Railways is unequivocally accepted, as has been done in respect of other railways of the world, Indian Railways will continue to remain a sun set railway. (For a fuller discussion on this subject please see my paper 'In Pursuit of a Productive Relationship').[1]

Apprehensions have sometimes been expressed regarding the possibility of Indian Railways exploiting its monopolistic position to earn extraordinary profit at least in commodities and sectors having poor elasticity of demand. It is often argued that most of the goods which Indian Railways carry such as

---

[1] K. B. Verma, 'In Pursuit of a Productive Relationship', *Readings in Indian Railway Finance*, ed. K. B. Verma, Academic Foundation, India, 1998.

coal, iron ore, cement, fertilizers etc. are intermediate goods and have a largely inelastic demand. And any increase in freight for these commodities will have cost multiplier effect on the finished products. Therefore, their transportation cost must be kept low. These apprehensions have turned out to be true, but for a different reason. Much to its dislike, Indian Railways has been forced to raise freight tariffs beyond reasonable limits due to its inability to raise passenger tariffs. The harmful effects of this are too well known to be discussed over here. It is hoped that this is an aberration and a temporary phenomenon and that some semblance of sanity will be restored after the setting up of the Rail Tariff Regulatory Authority which is already under way.

But what do we exactly mean by 'commercialisation of railways'? Commercialisation in the context of Indian Railways implies freedom, within the law of the land, to

- invest in and carry out such activities which promise financial return in excess of capital and operating costs of the activity
- increase profitable activities as well as curtail such activities which do not yield profit or at least cover its costs
- raise resources, both financial as well as physical, from the least cost and most efficient sources
- produce what is demanded by the customer backed by his willingness to pay
- rationalise its manpower and compensation policies to suit its requirements
- fix tariffs which enable it to sell its products at profit.

But, freedom is not a one-sided coin. In a utopian *laissez faire* fully competitive economy, the sternest disciplinarians are the market forces of demand and supply. Elimination from the market is the price of failure. But railway industry, due to its huge sunk costs (the contestability theory), is not a competitive industry and railways everywhere are so entwined with all activities of the economy and social lives of the people that they cannot be allowed to fail. Hence, where railways are not government owned, the governments have undertaken the role of guiding the affairs of railways through various regulatory measures. In India too setting up a Rail Tariff Regulatory Authority has been recently announced. But regulating tariffs is only part of the issue. Many other aspects of railway working would need to be regulated. It has, therefore, been suggested elsewhere in this book that the role of this Regulatory Authority should be widened to include other regulatory functions as well.

Generally two measures are suggested to impart the character of a commercial enterprise to Indian Railways viz. corporatising it and compensating it for the cost of Public Service Obligations. It has been argued in this book that this is not only inadequate; it is unworkable without other supporting measures. Commercialisation is a multidimensional problem. The steps required to be taken for commercialisation, particularly of an organisation like the Indian Railways which is strongly cast in the mould of a government department, have to be much more pervasive.

The next point to be considered is: How will commercialisation help the users and the economy, which actually is the purpose of any reform. It is expected that commercialisation in the true sense, will

- free the railways from undesirable external influence in its decision-making process
- provide clear organisational focus
- help in rationalising fares and freights and services
- help raise resources for expansion, modernisation and providing better service
- instil greater financial discipline and cut costs
- enable better investment decisions
- enable proper allocation of costs leading to more rational allocation of resources.

It must be clarified that commercialisation of Indian Railways in no way means that it cannot be used as a vehicle for discharging the Public Service Obligation of the government. There is no apparent contradiction between the two. In fact, railways everywhere and at all times have been among the best agencies for providing such benefits by the government. It only means that the two, i.e., the commercial nature of Railways and Public Service Obligations of the government should not be mixed up. Railways can certainly be made to carry out Public Service Obligations on behalf of the government, but it should be on commercial terms like any other service.

Some important measures required to be taken for commercialisation of Indian Railways are described subsequently.

Corporatisation

There were three fundamental recommendations of the Acworth Committee (1921).

- The Railway budget should be separated from the General Budget of the Government of India.
- Railways should make a fixed annual payment to General Revenues which should be linked to investment by Government of India in Railways.
- There should be an arm's length relationship between the government and Railways.

The first two have been successfully implemented. The last one has not even been attempted for more than ninety years. Railways in India are the richest source for distributing power, pelf, patronage and employment to the favourites. In fact, the bear hug has become much tighter after Independence.

The first essential step in the direction of commercialisation of Indian Railways is its corporatisation. This route has been followed by all other railways of the world. In India also all experts have repeatedly recommended that the only way to minimise (altogether elimination being impossible) the role of both government bureaucracy whose 'officials are not qualified either by training or experience to judge the essentially commercial and technical question where and when the circumstances of a railway undertaking justify bold undertaking of large sums, having regard not merely to the actual condition of the physical machine at the moment, but to the prospects of development and the requirement of the future (Acworth Committee)' as well as political influence in Railways, is to convert Indian Railways into a Corporation. Railways must be freed from the trammels of being a government department. Commercial functioning and a government departmental structure are contradiction in terms. The very nature of government precludes any scope for flexibility and agility required by a commercial organisation.

> While I reject privatisation as a solution for improving the productive efficiency of Indian Railways, there is much to be said in favour of changing their structure from a departmental undertaking into an independent public corporation. The establishment of such a corporation, if properly structured and armed with adequate powers for making decisions on such key variables as pricing and investment, would in my view, provide the management of Railways the necessary freedom to run their operations on sound commercial principles.[2]

---

[2] M. Q. Dalvi, 'Should Indian Railways Be Privatised', *Readings in Indian Railway Finance*, ed. K. B. Verma, Academic Foundation, India, 1998.

Once Indian Railways is converted into a corporation, it would be able to:

- take more rational investment decisions based purely on market demand.
- fix competitive tariffs based on the cost of service and value of service principles.
- deploy staff on considerations of cost, efficiency and productivity.
- fix its own conditions of service, remunerations and incentives for its employees.
- at a later date, enable government to off-load a part of its stake in the market as in case of many Public Sector Undertakings such as CONCOR Rites, NTPC, SAIL, Coal India, many Banks etc. thereby raise much needed resources for investment purposes.
- relieve government of the responsibility of funding railway investments thereby release resources for other purposes.
- compel railways to follow stricter financial discipline.

The statement that corporatisation will compel railways to follow stricter financial discipline needs a little elaboration. This will happen because of four reasons.

- At present, since railways is a government department, its cheques have the backing of the government and do not bounce for want of balance in its bank account. This leads to all-round complacency. Efforts made in the past to implement stricter exchequer control have not met with much success. After corporatisation, railways will lose this backing and its cheques will run the risk of bouncing for want of funds. This will force railways to remain within its means.
- Its investment decisions will have to be made with much greater care and caution and projects executed with much greater speed.
- Rationalisation of staff which accounts for more than 50 per cent of the operation and maintenance cost will become unavoidable.
- Implementation of a revised Incentive Scheme as described in Chapter 12 will further aid stricter financial discipline.

It must be emphasised that corporatisation is the unavoidable first step towards commercialisation. No other measure can succeed without it.

But corporatisation alone is not adequate. It will only be a halfway house. It is also rightly said that corporatisation alone will not reduce political interference either, as is commonly seen in the case of the public sector undertakings in India at present. This phenomenon is again not unique to India. Mere corporatisation did not help in reducing political interference in railway matters in other countries also. As mentioned earlier, conversion of Japanese Railways into a fully government-owned Corporation in 1949, in no way helped to reduce government control or political influence in railways.

At least four more steps need to be taken to make corporatisation effective and reap the benefits of commercialisation, viz.

- separation of policy from execution
- the government playing the true role of a shareholder
- induction of Independent Members into the Railway Board
- creating an appropriate motivation mechanism.

The first three measures are aimed at creating as much arm's length relationship as possible between government and railways with Indian Railways still remaining within the folds of the Government of India. And the last one aims to create a stake of all the employees in the financial success of the organisation.

Remaining within the folds of the government has been useful to the railways in its day-to-day ground-level operation. It helps in obtaining better cooperation from other government departments and civic authorities in times of need, which it may not be able obtain as a purely private company.

The first two measures viz. separation of policy from execution and the government acquiring the role of a shareholder, are discussed below and the other two measures are discussed in Chapters 11 and 12, respectively.

Separation of policy, execution and regulation

At present, the Ministry of Railways has a dual role. It acts as government in the form of Ministry of Railways as well as the executive body in the form of the Railway Board. Actually it discharges three functions – policy making, execution of the policy and regulatory function. Some have argued that such a structure enables quicker decisions. It may theoretically appear to be so. But there is no empirical evidence to provc or disprove such an assertion. But it surely is something like 'I'll be judge and I'll be jury, …, I'll try the whole case and condemn you to death' of Alice in Wonderland.

Assigning the three functions, which are entirely different in nature but impinge upon each other, to one body leads to mixing up of roles and dilution of responsibilities. A parallel may be drawn with the legislative, executive and judicial functions of a government. There must be clear-cut distinction between the three functions and each function should be assigned to three different entities. It is only then that each may be able to execute its functions satisfactorily and be held clearly accountable for the success or failure of the responsibilities assigned to it.

In the case of Indian Railways, for example, whether or not providing a rail link to Jammu and Kashmir or to the North East or to carry students at concessional rates or running suburban trains at depressed fares as measures of social welfare or constructing and operating railway lines for strategic reasons are matters of state policy. Whether the Railways need to enhance its capacity to meet the developmental needs of the economy, rather than on commercial considerations, is also a matter of policy. Such decisions should rightfully be taken by the policy framing wing of the government, not its executing wing, i.e., the railways. At present, major investment decisions are taken by the Planning Commission and the Ministry of Finance on a host of considerations not always on commercial considerations. But its consequences are borne by the railways.

Executing policies should be the responsibility of the non-policy formulating body – irrespective of whether Indian Railways is corporatized or not. And the policy-making body should be able to provide the resources for execution of those policies. In this respect, the German model described in Chapter 8 is of considerable relevance.

Such a structure is possible only by separating the policy-making body from the executing body.

Therefore,

- The Ministry of Railways should be abolished and the policy making function regarding railways should be assigned to a separate body, say the Ministry of Transport for example. In fact, the function of policy and planning for all modes of transport such as roads, railways, airports and sea ports need to be concentrated in one single body to enable a better coordinated approach towards the total transport needs of the country.

  Such examples exist in other countries also, e.g., the Ministry of Land, Infrastructure and Transport in Japan. The Ministry of

Railways in Russia was renamed as the Federal Rail Transport Agency (FTRA) and made responsible for exercising regulatory functions, implementing the reform programme as well as licensing of federal railway activities, but not running the railways. In China policy and planning relating to railways has been assigned to the Ministry of communication.

- Indian Railways should be converted into a wholly government-owned corporation, say the Indian Railway Corporation (IRC), and entrusted with the task of executing the policy laid down by the Ministry of Transport. Later in this book it has been suggested that after corporatisation, part of the shares of Indian Railways Corporation should be divested to raise funds for investment purposes.
- Further, since policy making is not a day-to-day function, the Ministry of Transport should in no way exercise a controlling influence on railways.
- The relationship between the government and Railway Corporation should be governed by a concretised actionable Memorandum of Understanding.
- The regulatory function should be assigned to a Rail Regulatory Authority entrusted with the task of ensuring that fares and freights charged are fair to the customers and adequate to ensure the financial health of railways, safety practices are followed, ensuring that the government is fair to the railways and is complying with the commitments made by it. The Regulatory Authority will also carry out the function presently carried out by commissioner of Railway Safety. It must also ensure that the Indian Railway Corporation is sincerely and successfully implementing the terms of the MOU. An important task of the Authority will be to arbitrate between the government and the Railways, should the need arise to do so.

The Rail Tariff Regulatory Authority which is proposed to be set up should itself be converted into a Rail Regulatory Authority. It should be assigned with all the regulatory functions described above including regulation of tariffs. Needless to say, it should be an independent authority. It should not be a judicial body but a quasi-judicial body. Besides the judicial Member, it will be important to include persons familiar with railway working.

Similar three-way separation of functions relating to Indian Railways has been recommended by the Rakesh Mohan Committee (2001) also.

Memorandum of Understanding

After the separation of policy from execution, the bedrock of relationship between the government and railways should be a Memorandum of Understanding (MOU). The MOU, for example, should

- define and concretise government requirement regarding new lines, running of passenger or freight trains, services to be provided etc.
- lay down policies regarding continuing with or discounting unviable lines and services.
- costs to be borne by the government.
- financial and other resources to be provided by the government.
- targets to be adhered by the railways in respect of timeline of projects, cost of projects, volume of freight and passenger traffic.
- performance parameters regarding quality of service provided by Railways.
- financial targets for Railways such as with regard to revenue, costs and profits.

The above list is purely illustrative just to convey the idea, not exhaustive. Obviously, the actual framework has to be worked out by the concerned parties such as railway officials, government officials and legal experts.

The very purpose of MOU is to create as much distance as possible between the government and railways and permit Railways the freedom and flexibility to operate as a commercial enterprise. Therefore, temptation to micro-manage railways through the MOU route must be avoided. The emphasis should be on output rather than on micro issues such as speed of trains, manpower management, administrative structures, selection and posting of senior management personnel etc.

While at present it may not be feasible to permit Railways to follow its own employee compensation policies, it should be aimed at as soon as practicable. As a commercial enterprise IR should also have commercial compensation policy – say for example a two-part pay structure as is the norm in the private sector, a fixed pay and performance related variable pay, cost to the company (CTC) principle rather than a myriad of allowances and so on.

The MOU should be an annual feature and subject to periodical review between the Ministry of Transport, Rail Regulatory Authority and Railways. Even now there is the practice of the government entering into MOUs with the public sector undertakings through the Department of Public Enterprises.

An important outcome of the MOU scheme would be the elimination of the need to have a separate Railway Budget. This needs a little elaboration.

There were two reasons for separating Railway Budget from the General Budget in 1924.

One was to protect the General Budget from the uncertainties of railway revenues which formed major part of revenues of the Government of India and was much dependent upon the vagaries of the monsoons. This situation does not exist anymore as railway revenues form only a small percentage of the revenues of the Government of India.

The second purpose was to provide fiscal independence to railways to operate as a commercial concern. This purpose has been totally defeated. It is true that Railways enjoy far greater operational and financial independence compared to other government departments. But that is not the issue. The issue is whether the existing nature and extent of independence is enough to enable Railways to function as a commercial enterprise. In this respect, the separation of Railway Budget has failed to meet its purpose. A well-designed and balanced MOU along with a Regulatory Authority in place is more likely to achieve the required freedom and flexibility.

Therefore, the justification for having a separate Railway Budget gets considerably weakened. However, since Railways will continue to be owned by the government, policy matters regarding Railways and government receipts from and expenditure on Railways would still have to continue to be a part of the General Budget as at present, though via the Ministry of Transport. It would then be the responsibility of the Ministry of Transport to obtain the approval of Parliament for its policies and expenses regarding Railways like other modes of transport. Having a separate Railway Budget would then not be necessary.

Another fall-out of corporatizing Indian Railways and the MOU mechanism would be the role of the Financial Commissioner. At present, the FC has a dual role. While he/she is the head of the Finance wing of Indian Railways, he/she is also the representative of the Minister of Finance in the Ministry of Railways. In the changed structure, since the relationship between Railways and the government will be governed through an MOU, his/her being the representative of Minister of Finance in Railways will not only be superfluous but will also be in conflict with the interest of Railways. Hence, the FC should no longer be regarded as representative of the Minister of Finance in Railways and expected to keep the Minister of Finance informed of the affairs of Railways.

Since the MOU is expected to acquire the nature of a contract between the government and Railways, there has to be a mechanism to deal with failure to honour the contract by both parties and provisions for resolution of disputes. As mentioned above, this would legitimately fall within the responsibility of the Railway Regulatory Authority.

The MOU mechanism is designed to give Railways the character of a private enterprise without actually privatising it. It has the merit of clearly defining the roles and responsibilities of both the government and Railways and can be the most potent mechanism for reducing external influences in the affairs of Railways.

Government as shareholder

The Acworth Committee (1921) as well as the Convention Committee, 1949 unequivocally declared the Government of India as the owner and single shareholder of railways. But in practice the actual role of government has become that of debtor-owner rather than that of shareholder-owner.

A reference to history will help. Unlike the normal capital structure of a commercial concern consisting of both debt and equity, the Acworth Committee made the entire financing by Government of India as debt. It has continued like this since then. However, this must be viewed in the context of the situation prevailing at that time and the purpose sought to be achieved by such a structure. The predominant concern of the Committee was to ensure a predictable income from Railways to the Government of India. Logically, this could be achieved only by treating the entire investment as debt, entitled to a predetermined return. If a part or whole of it had been treated as equity, the same uncertainty of revenue to the government would have continued, defeating the very purpose of the Committee. Therefore, making government investment entirely as debt was the only course open to the Committee.

It is important to emphasise that it was the 'certainty' element of the return which was more important than its 'quantum'. This becomes clear from the recommendations of the Convention Committee, 1924, which went a step further than the Acworth Committee. The Acworth Committee had recommended a rate of Dividend equal to the rate at which the government raised loans for financing investment in railways. But the Convention Committee of 1924 fixed a much lower rate of Dividend but added a variable element to it as well. It recommended a fixed return of only 1 per cent of capital invested plus a variable return of one-fifth of any surplus profit remaining after payment of the fixed return. This gave government investment in railways a dual character – debt as well as equity, fixed return as well as variable return, a composition which can be well made use of even today.

At the end of 2011–12, Indian Railway's debt to the Government of India was to the tune of ₹ 1,61,447.97. The 'Expert Group For Modernisation of Railways' (February 2012)[3] has estimated an investment requirement of ₹ 5,60,395 Crs. in addition to ₹ 4,42,744 Crs. of investment estimated by the Railway sub-group for the Twelfth Five Year Plan during the next five years. A large, though not all, part of it will have to be financed by loan from the government. With such large investments projected in future, the Dividend liability is bound to become crippling unless the Railway Convention Committees in future take a philanthropically lenient view. It is apprehended that railways may not be able to bear this burden and land itself in a debt trap.

It is also relevant to mention that the Railway Convention Committee, 2004 (Report No. 112) had estimated that Railways had already paid a Dividend of ₹ 49,306 Crs., i.e., 77.96 per cent of the capital-at-charge up to 2007–08. Thus, quite a substantial part of the principal has already been recovered by the government.

The only practicable solution, therefore, is for the government to play its role as a shareholder and convert the entire amount invested in Railways, i.e. capital-at-charge as at present into equity. This is justified not only on grounds of providing relief to railways but is also in keeping with commercial principles. The 'Expert Group on Capital Structure of Indian Railways' (1978)[4] had gone to the extent of suggesting a 'write off' of the contribution made till then by the government. It is hard to find examples of a commercial concern depending entirely on debt capital. None of the public sector undertakings of the Government of India also is burdened with interest paying debt in perpetuity.

It would be seen from the survey of reforms on other railways that one of the important actions taken by the governments in those countries including China was to relieve the railways from the burden of past debt so that they could start from afresh.

---

[3] 'Expert Group For Modernisation of Railways', February 2012. www. prsindia.org/administration/upload/general, March 14, 2012

[4] 'Expert Group on the Capital Structure of Indian Railways' (1978), Railway Fare and Freight Committee the Report, (Decemeber, 1993) Volume 1 Page 48.

The suggestion regarding conversion of the existing debt into equity may seem to lead to a loss of revenue to the government as it involves surrendering a well-known source of certain income. But this may not necessarily be so. The government would still be entitled to a share of profits in railways. Further, financial relief to railways will help improve service quality, expansion of network which will have multiplier effect on economic activity. This will lead to mopping up more revenue through various taxes. Not to mention other unquantifiable social benefits.

Even if it means some loss of revenue to the government, it is not too great a sacrifice considering the extent to which some foreign governments have gone in supporting their railways in view of the socio-economic benefit of railways.

After conversion of the Government of India investment into equity, the debt: equity ratio would no doubt become temporarily lopsided. But with the measures proposed below it will soon get corrected.

- All further funds from Government of India (GOI) should be treated as commercial debt. This will in due course lead to a balanced capital structure of both debt and equity which is the norm in commercial concerns.
- Loan from GOI should be project specific. Since the loan would be project specific, the rate charged should not be the Average Borrowing Rate of the government but should be the same as the rate actually paid by GOI for raising such project specific loan plus a nominal administrative charge, which should not be more than that paid by Railways to IRFC.
- The loan, like other commercial loans, should be a repayable one just as the lease charges paid to IRFC includes an element of capital repayment. This will eventually make Indian Railways debt-free.

No doubt the suggestions of raising of loan by Railways from the market, or paying interest to the government at a rate equal to the rate paid by government for loans raised specifically for Railways instead of Dividend (whose rate is currently much lower than the market rate) and the loan being a repayable loan, would increase the cost of capital and have consequential effect on tariffs.

The governments where railway reforms have taken place, particularly Germany and Sweden, got around this problem in the following manner.

- Where construction of new lines is taken up by the railway on commercial considerations (such as project lines and port lines in

India) railway is responsible for meeting all costs including capital cost. Where new line construction is required by the government as a part of its transport policy, the government meets the cost of capital.
- Where local suburban services are required by the local bodies, they meet the entire cost and retain the earnings from them.

These aspects should form an essential part of MOU between the Ministry of Transport and the Indian Railway Corporation.

Looked from another angle, it is unclear as to whether cheap capital available to Railways from government is all that good. Is it advisable to suppress the true cost of a capital expenditure or for that matter any expenditure?

In fact, where management has no direct personal stake in profits, cheap capital may work to the detriment of the company.[5] It may lead to complacency and misallocation of resources. On the other hand true market cost of capital will enable a clearer picture to emerge regarding the actual cost of a particular project, and enforce greater discipline in project formulation and decision making. This will be to the long-term benefit of Railways as well as the country.

It needs to be kept in mind that Railways is already faced with depending more and more on expensive capital from the market due to the strained financial position of the government. It has, therefore, to get used to the idea of expensive capital for investment.

However, converting debt into shares is only one aspect of the issue.

> .... If the equity capital of the proposed Railway Corporation were entirely held by the Central Government, control over the operation of the Railway would be no different from the existing ministerial control and bureaucratic intervention. Such a system would not be conducive to injecting commercial procedures and market discipline into the management of Indian Railways. An important and innovative breakthrough in the structural model of public corporation in India would be to invite private sector to freely participate in their equity base...... the same structural model should be adopted for the Railway Corporation by inviting private investors initially to purchase 20% of the Corporation's capital, but gradually this share should be raised to 49%. This will still leave the control of the Railways with the Central Government, if so desired.[6]

---

[5] K. B. Verma, 'In Pursuit of a Productive Relationship', *Readings in Indian Railway Finance*, ed. K. B. Verma, Academic Foundation, India, 1998.

[6] M. Q. Dalvi, 'Should Indian Railways Be Privatised', *Readings in Indian Railway Finance*, ed. K. B. Verma, Academic Foundation, India, 1998.

Thus, in order to take full advantage of conversion of debt into equity, not only the debt should be converted into equity but a part of it should be off-loaded into the market, as has been done in the case of CONCOR a public sector undertaking of Railways and many other undertakings of the Government of India such as SAIL, NTPC, Power Grid Corporation, State Bank of India, Indian Overseas Bank, Allahabad Bank to name just a few.

This will obviously require the Railway Corporation to be listed with the stock exchange.

Divesting a part of the shares of the Railway Corporation will have the added benefit of raising quite a substantial amount of capital for investment in Railways from other than government sources, relieving the pressure on the general revenues and enabling the government to increase its financing of social sector schemes like health, education etc. as well as on other economic activities. Once the railway shares are off-loaded and traded, the share values will exert further pressure on Railways to perform well.

Primacy of commercial function

This is decidedly an essential requirement for inculcating a commercial culture,

It is quite difficult to conceive of an organisation which professes to be a commercial organisation but ascribes to the commercial function a secondary importance, or rather not even a secondary importance.

At present, the Member Traffic in the Railway Board looks after both the functions – Operations and Commercial. But from zonal level downwards the two functions get separated into two different branches viz. Operating and Commercial and for all intent and purposes are treated as two separate departments.

Historically, the Operation function has had a pre-eminent position in Indian Railways, so much so that the officers posted in the Commercial Department are often considered somewhat inferior to those posted in the Operating Department. To get posted in the Operating Department is often regarded as a matter of prestige.

The primacy of the operating function was necessary when Railways were the prime carriers and did not face any problem of demand. The main problem in Railways then was on the supply side, i.e., supply of wagons to the customers and movement of trains. All other functions were only supportive to the operating function. In the now changed market conditions, this is not so anymore. The problem is on the demand side, attracting traffic to rail. Particularly, in view of the fact that with the increasing introduction of computerised methods of rolling stock management, crew management, train movement management etc. a large part of the operating functions can be computerised. Computerised train operations management is no longer considered something exotic. It has been in existence in many railways for decades. The computerised Total Operating System (TOPS) was implemented in Canadian Pacific Railway sometime in the late 1970s. Though terribly lagging behind, in India as well the operating function, like so many other functions, is being computerised and some modules have already been rolled out. Thus, in the changed circumstances operations management does not call for as much personal attention, monitoring and management as it used to do earlier.

Therefore, the primacy of the operating function has become anachronistic.

On the other hand, the commercial function is facing more and more intense competition from other modes of transport. It has become much more challenging. It requires great personal skill, initiative, innovation and involvement. In an economy where suppliers of transport, or for that matter any product, have to compete for the love and affection of consumers, the commercial function, particularly, marketing and sales, has come to acquire critical importance.

Therefore, it is imperative that the primacy of the commercial function be recognised and be given the importance it deserves. And persons especially suited should be selected and trained in relevant skills and then be posted to the Commercial department. In fact, time has come when the wide difference between the commercial function and the operating function, already existing in practice, is recognised and the *de facto* divide between the two branches of the Traffic department be formalised by splitting the two right from top to bottom.

The commercial function is so important that nothing less than the creation of a separate post of Member Commercial in Railway Board will do. The post of Member Traffic should be split up. A new post of Member Commercial should be created and the post of Member Traffic should be re-designated as Member Operations. As suggested later in Chapter 11, recruitment for the commercial cadre should also be made separately.

The creation of a separate post of Member Commercial in the Board is highly desirable irrespective of whether Indian Railways is corporatised or not.

Division as Business Unit

Indian Railways follows a three-tier administrative structure but only a two-tier business structure. The three-tier administrative structure is – the Railway Board, the zonal railways and the Divisions. And the two-tier business structure is – the Railway Board and the zonal railways. The smallest business unit is a railway zone. A railway zone is a business unit in the sense that it is a profit centre. The Operating Ratio and Profit and Loss statement of each railway zone is separately compiled. It is thus possible to find out how well or otherwise a zone is performing financially. A Division is not a business unit in the sense that Operating Ratio and Profit and Loss statement are not compiled for the Divisions. As a consequence, it is not possible to find out the financial performance of a Division.

This kind of business unit structure has a direct bearing on the financial management of Railways. A railway zone is too large. Hence, zonal financial performance gives too macro a picture for any meaningful financial management. Therefore, it is time Indian Railways adopt a more micro-level structure for its financial management, i.e., treat Divisions as identifiable business units. Each Division in Indian Railways is quite a large unit by itself. Each Division employs between 20,000 and 25,000 staff and has a budget of more than a thousand crore Rupees or so which is bigger than that of many companies. With increasing emphasis on financial performance, it is important that each Division is treated as a business unit in its own right.

Earlier it was impractical to compile Operating Ratio and Profit and Loss for the Divisions because of the huge manual calculation that it would have involved. With increasing use of computers it is now possible to do so.

For a unit to be treated as a Business Unit, it would require its costs, revenues and profits to be compiled separately. At present, almost all costs of a Division are compiled by the Division. The main difficulty lies in compiling its earnings. At present, the Divisions compile what is called its 'originating earnings'. But this is not its true earnings. Its true earnings would be the 'apportioned earnings', on account of traffic originating or terminating on the Division as well as traffic passing through it. Unfortunately, it is this calculation of apportioned earnings for a Division which is the main problem.

At present, apportioned earnings are calculated for zonal railways only, through a computer programme based on an apportionment methodology. The methodology does not provide for Division-wise apportionment, probably because of the limited processing capability of the computers which existed when the apportionment programme was originally developed decades ago. Now that much more powerful computers are available, it is not difficult to upgrade the computer programme to incorporate Division-wise apportionment also. Once this is done and some further tweaking is done on the cost side, it is possible to compile its accounts separately and treat the Divisions as business units.

Treating a Division as a profit centre in no way implies that it has to be a net profit earning Division. Some Divisions are physically so located and their nature of traffic is such that while they have very high loading of freight, the lead of those traffic is very low on those Divisions. As a consequence, while they incur high terminal handling cost, they are unlikely to get much share of earnings on apportionment of earnings although some weightage is provided for terminal handling. Same in the case of primarily passenger-oriented Divisions or predominance of low fare paying passenger traffic and so on.

Even though all Divisions need not be net profit earning Divisions, even in their case such a compilation will help to identify the problem areas, create more financial awareness and enable much better financial management at the micro level. Further, as discussed in Chapter 12 on 'Incentive Scheme', it will also make it possible to have a more meaningful incentive scheme than the existing Productivity Linked Bonus Scheme.

For the purpose of better financial management it would have been definitely preferable to have even smaller business units than a Division. But at present since a Division is the smallest administrative unit on Indian Railways, it is not possible to have a smaller business unit.

Organisational culture

Organisational culture refers to the mindset of its employees. It develops over a period of time and is shaped by a host of factors such as the aims of the organisation, the mental make-up of the leadership, expectations of the employees, the environment in which it operates and so on. It gets ingrained into every fibre of the organisation. The irony is that very seldom the insiders are able to perceive its warts and accept that perhaps there may be something wrong and needs to change. And since it is basically a mental phenomenon, resistance to change is the highest. But unless the organisational culture is aligned with the goals of the organisation and expectations from it, the chances of success of the organisation are very remote.

If Indian Railways is to function as a commercial enterprise, the mindset of the people must be tuned accordingly.

This is as true of Indian Railways as any other railway or for that matter any other organisation. That is why dynamic business leaders place a lot of emphasis on moulding the thinking of their employees and usually find it most difficult to do so.

As far as Indian Railways is concerned, there are two basic traits of a railwayman's mental make-up.

- The micro view. Concern only with the performance of one's own department or Division, disregarding its effect on the performance of Railways as a whole or the interest of the customer. An example will help to clarify the point. For ages, the midnight balance of wagons in a Division is considered an important performance criterion of the Division. The aim is to have as small balance of wagon holdings as possible at midnight. Lower the balance better it is. It shows that the Division has been able to flush out all the wagons it has received, hence performed well. This often leads to situations where Divisions tend to block the entry of goods trains from the adjoining Divisions into their own division unless they are confident of moving them out by midnight. The effect of this culture on the consignment and customer satisfaction needs no further explanation. It is, perhaps, a hangover of the days when the main problem of Railways was supply of rolling stock and movement of trains in a supplier's market, a world which has long gone by.
- Much more damaging is thinking in terms of physical performance only. Financial considerations occupy the lowest, if any, position in the minds of railwaymen. It is harsh but true that most of the Heads of Departments consider financial matters below their dignity. On the contrary, ignorance of and disdain for all things dealing with railway finances is worn as a badge of pride. So much so that their budgets are prepared not even by an officer of their department but by the Budget Babu (clerk). The singular contribution of the Head of the Department being the signature at the bottom of the page. And in almost all the monthly co-ordination meetings whether in the Divisions or in the zonal Head Offices, financial matters are discussed, if at all, towards the end, just in passing.

This culture has arisen from four factors:

- The existence of an easy route to avoid financial crisis just by reducing the Appropriation to Depreciation Reserve Fund.
- The possibility of the Railway Convention Committee coming to its rescue by reducing the rate of Dividend.
- Deferring payment of Dividend.
- The confidence that being a departmental undertaking, the government will ultimately bail out the Railways in times of crisis.

In such a situation the financial woes of Indian Railways is hardly surprising.

Lack for concern for financial matters is true not only of Indian Railways but elsewhere as well. The Lord Beecham report 'The Reshaping of British Railways' (1963) adversely commented on engineering driven rather than finance-driven culture of British Railways.

Recently, a World Bank Report on British Rail had this to say:

> The management structure of BR had been typical of the traditional, monolithic and production-driven railway. The basic management unit was the Regional General Manager ..... who had essentially full operating control over their area of the railway, but who had a cost, not a Net Revenue, objective.[7]

While the Regional General Managers in British Rail had at least a 'cost objective' railwaymen in India have neither a cost nor a revenue objective. Sole concern is with movement of trains to the almost complete obscurity of other considerations. The linking of Productivity Linked Bonus to Traffic Units (i.e., Net Tonne Kilometres) alone is ample testimony of this phenomenon.

The biggest challenge in Indian Railways, therefore, would be to change the mindset of railwaymen – to introduce a commercial culture, to think in terms of revenue and costs and profits. How to do it is outside the scope of this book. However, apart from massive repeated indoctrination drive over a period of time, particularly at the top echelons of the management, three steps are most likely to help in introducing commercial culture in Indian Railways viz. (i) according primacy to the Commercial function, (ii) recasting of PLB formulae to include all categories of employees and (iii) giving suitable weightage to financial performance in the incentive scheme.

---

[7] Louis S. Thompson, 'Privatising British Railways : Are There Lessons for World Bank and its Borrowers', World Bank 2004.

While the first one has been already dealt with above, the other two will be dealt with in Chapter 12 on Incentive Scheme.

Indian Railways cannot think of deliverance without making fundamental change in its mindset to bring financial considerations into its thinking. And the surest way to make someone think in terms of revenue, cost and profit is to link his rewards to profit.

Public Service Obligations

It is rightly said that IR suffers from a split personality disorder. On the one hand, it is seen as a government department and is expected to shoulder certain Social Service Obligations. On the other, it is seen as a commercial organisation and hence expected to be financially self-sufficient.

Traditionally, governments all over the world have always regarded railways both as a commercial enterprise as well as a vehicle for carrying out the government's Social Service Obligations. By their very nature railways are eminently suitable to carry out social service agenda of the government – providing transport service even in remote areas where railway operations may not be financially viable, carrying passengers at below cost for economically weaker sections of the society, charging reduced freight on export traffic to facilitate exports or charging reduced freight on certain commodities, such as coal or raw material, to promote balanced regional growth etc. In fact, railway services and Public Service Obligations cannot and need not be completely divorced from each other.

Both theoretically as well as practically there is nothing to debar a commercial undertaking being made to carry out social welfare activities in furtherance of government objectives. The problem arises when railways are expected to carry them at below cost and simultaneously remain financially viable. Many governments of the world have recognised the conflict and as described earlier, solved the problem in different ways.

The problem is quite acute in Indian Railways. The cost of Social Service Obligations borne by the railways since 2000–01 is shown in Table 10.1.

Table 10.1: Social service obligatiions (₹ Crs)

Year	*SSO*	*GTR*	*% to GTR*	*TWE*	*% to TWE*
2000–01	3283	34880	9.4	34662	9.5
2001–02	3948	37838	10.4	36293	10.9

Contd.

Contd.

Year	*SSO*	*GTR*	*% to GTR*	*TWE*	*% to TWE*
2002–03	3908	41068	9.5	38026	10.3
2003–04	3839	42905	8.9	39482	9.7
2004–05	5738	47370	12.1	42759	13.4
2005–06	4108	54491	7.5	45292	9
2006–07	3731	62732	5.9	49047	7.6
2007–08	4610	71720	6.4	54462	8.5
2008–09	11478	79862	14.4	71839	16
2009–10	14976	86964	17.2	82915	18.1
2010–11	15714	94356	16.6	89474	17.6
2011–12	17651	104110	17	98667	17.9

Note: SSO is Social Service Obligations; GTR is Gross Traffic Receipts; TWE is Total Working Expenditure
Source: Compiled by author

The problem becomes clearer in the form of a graph (Chart 10.1).

Chart 10.1: Social Service Obligation of Indian Railways

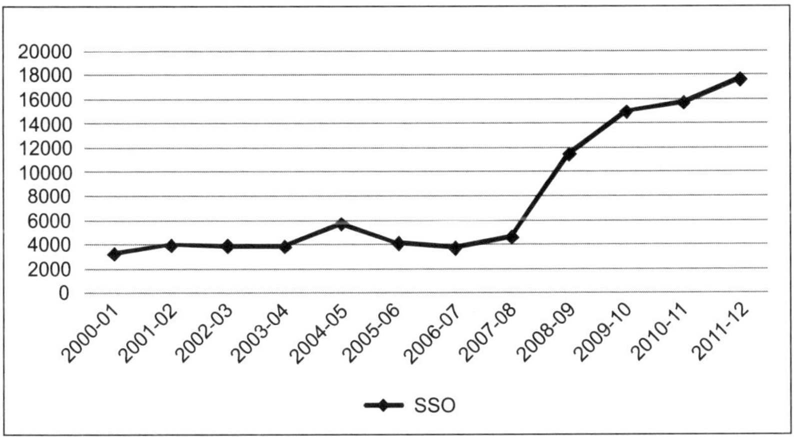

In terms of absolute figures the cost of Social Service Obligations in 2011–12 was a stupendous ₹ 17,651 Crs. These costs as percentages of Gross Traffic Receipts and Total Working Expenses are still more worrisome (Chart 10.2).

The sudden spurt in the cost of Social Service Obligation from 2008–09 was as a result of the pay hike after the Sixth Pay Commission. But even without the

Sixth Pay Commission the losses were more than 9 per cent, even 13 per cent in 2004–05. By all stretch of imagination these costs are too high. Compare this to the non-mandatory provision of Companies Act, 2013 requiring the corporate bodies to spend 2 per cent of their profits on corporate social responsibility.

Chart 10.2: Ratio of Social Service Obligation

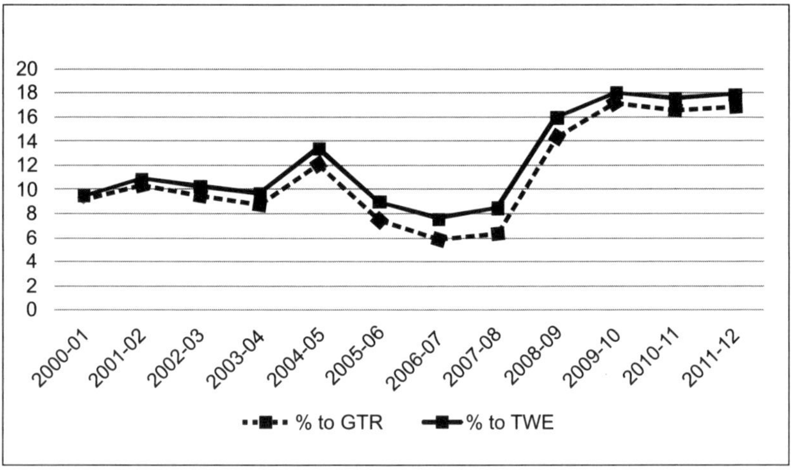

These figures are sometimes disputed. It is argued that since the traffic costing methodology followed by Indian Railways is far from perfect, it would not be correct to place much credence on the figures of losses. Some time back a committee was set up by the Railway Convention Committee (1991) to go into this question and estimate the amount of losses. The committee arrived at a different figure, though not too far from the losses estimated by IR. This is not surprising. Different studies are bound to come up with different estimates depending on the method adopted. And all methods can be defended or disputed depending upon one's predilections. It is impossible to say which method is correct. For the present analysis, the absolute figures are not as much important as the principle of it. Once the principles are agreed, it would not be difficult to come up with a reasonable methodology and compute the cost of Social Service Obligations accordingly.

In Indian Railways the main reason for losses are on account of losses in coaching services. The breakup of the main items on which Railways incur losses in passenger services are:

- Suburban services.
- Low fares in ordinary second class.

- Non-suburban commuters availing season tickets constituting about 25 per cent of non-suburban traffic.
- Season tickets on suburban services constituting 65% of the suburban traffic.
- Concession fares to various categories such as - student concession, senior citizen concession, recipients of gallantry awards, National Sports Awards, participants in national and state tournaments, Shram awards, war widows, patients suffering from cancer, tuberculosis and other serious diseases, handicapped persons, press correspondents, film technicians etc.
- Concessions extended to military traffic, postal traffic, transportation of seeds, milk, traffic to North East, material transported for emergency relief to areas affected by floods, droughts, cyclones, earthquake etc.

It can certainly be said that IR is subsidising those organisation whose responsibility it is to provide these services and bear its cost.

It is not quite clear why the cost of students concession should not be borne by the Ministry of Education instead of the Railways, or the cost of concession to senior citizens be borne by the Ministry of Personnel and Social Welfare or the cost of concessions to sports persons by the Ministry of Sports. Similarly, the full cost of transporting military traffic and concessional fares to war widows by the Ministry of Defence or the postal traffic by the Postal department etc. These concessions not only deprive the Railways of much needed funds for safety works, quality improvement and development works, it suppresses the costs of one wing of the government at the cost of another wing of the government and leading to misallocation of resources. The allocative efficiency of the economy gets severely vitiated.

Of all the Public Service Obligations shouldered by the Railways the loss on account of sub-urban services falls in an entirely different category. Unlike other Public Service Obligations, it is an institutional issue. The beneficiaries of this facility can in no way be said to belong to economically depressed sections of society. They mostly belong to the middle class who cannot be said to be economically deprived. In many cases the cost of transport is reimbursed by their employers. Thus, the benefit of extremely low fares is reaped by the employers at the cost of Railways. Even otherwise the responsibility of providing local transport facility to its citizens should rest with the local authorities rather than with the Railways.

In this context it is important to recall the principle of 'User Pays' implemented by many governments. For example, in the reformed structure of German Railways if a particular line or service is required by a local or regional authority, that authority pays for the cost of the service, including the cost of infrastructure. In Sweden, the responsibility for running local commuter trains was transferred to County Passenger Transport Authority/ies (CPTAs). However, the CPTAs are entitled to a subsidy from the government for a period of ten years, the subsidy being equal to the loss previously being incurred by SJ on running those services. After ten years, the CPTAs will have to bear the cost of such services if they decide to continue with it.

Another important source of losses to railways on account of Public Service Obligations is operating losses on unviable branch lines. In 2011–12 there were 88 such lines estimated to account for the loss of ₹ 1366 Crs.

> 'Several high-level committees have unanimously recommended that all such uneconomic branch lines, where alternative modes of transport exist or can be developed should be closed down... . There is, however, reluctance on the part of state governments to close down such lines ... . The Railway Reforms Committee in Part XI of their report on 'Economics' (October 1983) had recommended that ...... where alternative road infrastructure could be developed, should be closed down and in cases where the state governments do not agree for closure for their reasons they should share the losses with the Railways on 50:50 basis...... the Railways are ready to offer financial assistance as under:
>
> (a) On one time basis, the Railways may subsidise the procurement of additional buses required due to closure of rail sections subject to the State Government agreeing for their permanent closure.
> (b) Again, on one time basis, Railways may offer financial assistance for development/improvement of road infrastructure which will be prerequisite for withdrawal of train services
> (c) Offer of Railway embankments in respect of 13 lines in Gujrat for conversion into all weather metalled road.'[8]

The above offers have been in existence for more than two decades but nothing has happened because of the reluctance of the state governments to permit railways to discontinue these lines. Their reluctance, understandably, arises partly from apprehension of its adverse political fallout but mostly from the fact that they do not have to bear its cost. The only way to compel the states

[8] Explanatory Memorandum to Railway Budget 2013–14, Appendix XXI.

to have a serious look at the problem and come up with an agreeable solution in consultation with Railways, would be to adjust the losses from the central funds transferred to the states according to the losses suffered in their areas.

The issue of Public Service Obligations need to be looked at from another angle – in terms of overall what the government gives to the Railways and what it gets from the Railways. The government gives only some funds in the form of non-repayable interest (called Dividend) earning loan to Railways for meeting part of its capital expenditure. The receipts of Government include Dividend. But it should also include the amounts (cost of Social Service Obligations and losses on uneconomic branch lines) which it should rightfully pay to railways although it does not do so at present. Table 10.2 shows this position for the last ten years.

Table 10.2 shows the capital contributed by the government in the concerned year i.e. Railway receipts from government on capital account. The column Dividend shows the payment by Railway to the government. The columns SSO and UBL show the loss to Railways which should have been compensated by the government. The total of these three elements Dividend, SSO and UBL should therefore, rightly be taken as receipt by government from Railways. The last column Net Contribution shows the difference between receipt by Railway from the government and the receipt by government from Railways in the concerned year.

Table 10.2: Net contribution by government (₹ Crs)

	Addl. Capital	*Dividend*	*SSO*	*UBL*	*Total to Govt*	*Net Contri.*
2000–01	3007	2131	3283	449	5863	-2856
2001–02	4096	2337	3948	434	6719	-2623
2002–03	3952	2665	3908	461	7034	-3082
2003–04	4963	3087	3839	410	7336	-2373
2004–05	3285	2716	5738	405	8859	-5574
2005–06	4705	3005	4108	451	7564	-2859
2006–07	4483	3584	3731	425	7740	-3257
2007–08	11254	4239	4610	422	9271	1983
2008–09	2839	4718	11478	732	16928	-14089
2009–10	15417	5543	14976	1198	21717	-6300

Note: SSO is Social Service Obligations; UBL is losses on Uneconomic Branch Lines
Source: Complied by author

In all years except in 2007–08 the Government has taken more from Railways than given to the Railways. The ill effects of this distorted situation are not difficult to appreciate.

The Ministry of Finance has confused the issue of Social Service Obligations on two counts.

On the question as to why the Railways should be asked to bear the cost of providing such services which are actually the obligations of other wings of the government, the Ministry of Finance stated before the Railway Convention Committee that

> From the Ministry of Finance we do not accept this argument. The whole purpose of Government is to undertake social obligations. All Public Sector Undertakings are in the Public Sector because they undertake social obligations.[9]

Obviously, the above argument misses the point. The issue is not whether Railways should or should not undertake such activities. The issue is as to who should pay for it? And why the Ministries or organisations whose responsibility it is to provide those service should not bear the cost of such services rather than Railways? The Ministry of Finance skirted the issue.

The next issue on which the Ministry of Finance has failed to appreciate the point relates to returns to the government. It has been argued by Railways that if the cost of Public Service Obligations borne by railways is added to the payment of Dividend, the cost of capital to Railways is extremely high, around 19% or so in 1989–90 and 14.44 per cent in 2011–12. It will become still higher if the losses on account of uneconomic branch lines are added to it.

The Ministry of Finance stated before the Railway Convention Committee that

> You cannot calculate the return to Government by how much social obligations that you have discharged. That would be a completely wrong method of accounting. It is not an accepted method of accounting for Government Undertakings. Railways is one of the largest Undertakings of the Government and on the social obligations the entire Government is committed to discharge it. This is not the proper way of calculating the return to Government[10]

---

[9] *Railway Convention Committee Report* (2004) Report No. 112.

[10] *Railway Convention Committee Report* (2004) Report No. 112.

The above statement is both correct and incorrect.

It is correct in the sense that such a calculation is actually not a formal part of accounting. It does not enter into accounts and, therefore, cannot be treated as a part of return to the government.

But the above argument again wholly misses the point at issue. The main contention of Railways is that since the government is not paying Railways for the cost of Social Service Obligations, it is saving that amount. Therefore, even though it does not enter into formal accounts, it is effectively a part of the return to the government, hence it should be considered as such.

In this context it is necessary to once again recall the observations of the Railway Convention Committee (1998) which very adversely commented on the practice of Railways being made to bear the cost of Public Service Obligations.

> Considering the budgetary support from General Exchequer being reduced from the level of 75% in the Fifth Plan to 23% in the Eighth Plan and the increasing dependence of the Railways on market borrowings, the Committee feel that any unilateral increase in the rate of Dividend without compensating the Indian Railways for carrying social obligations will only put additional pressure on the already strained Railway finances… . In this connection, the Committee wish to point out that on the basis of the recommendations made by the Railway Convention Committee (1991) in their Twelfth Report, an Inter-Ministerial Working Group consisting of representatives of Ministry of Railways, Ministry of Finance and Planning Commission was constituted to look into the social obligations borne by the Railways. The Working Group had submitted its unanimous Report in May, 1997 wherein the Social Service Obligation borne by Railways in 1994–95 was reassessed at ₹886 cr. The Committee are constrained to note with disapproval the attitude of the Ministry of Finance of not agreeing to the unanimous recommendation of the Working Group for compensating the Railways on this reduced scale. The Committee recommend that the unanimous recommendation of the Working Group to which the Ministry of Finance was also a party should be accepted without any further delay.

The Committee recommends that

> In order to give the Indian Railways a level playing field with other modes of transportation, the Indian Railways need to be compensated under various heads like losses incurred on transportation of essential commodities,

> subsidised movement to North Eastern States, operation of unremunerative lines, commuter services etc. The above losses should become explicit charges on the allocations made to the various Central Ministries of the Government to cover specific areas of social responsibility thereby relieving Railways of this burden in order to operate as a commercial enterprise.[11]

The government has, however, not agreed to the above recommendations.

It is not generally realised that apart from the direct financial effect of requiring railways to shoulder the cost of Public Service Obligations, its indirect effects are no less devastating.

- It blurs the organisational objective.
- Opens the door to political pressures to provide unviable services.
- By requiring Railways to bear these costs, the true cost of providing such services gets hidden leading to misallocation of resources.
- It facilitates Railways also to sweep its own inefficiencies under the carpet under the guise of public utility service.
- Poor financial results of Railways are often taken as a failure of Railways little realising that bearing costs of some other branch of the government is the major contributing factor for the poor results. Consistently poor financial results are bad for the image of any commercial concern and very demoralising.

If railways are to be treated as a commercial enterprise, the government and its different departments must be regarded as just other customers and they should be required to pay the same fares and freights like other customers. This, in fact, has been one of the corner stones of railway reform in all countries.

This is not to say that IR should not carry out any Public Service Obligation. But it should be limited to 2 per cent of its profit (calculated according to commercial accounting principles) as in the case of other commercial concerns.

[11] *Railway Convention Committee Report*, 1998.

11

Management Structure

The administrative framework of Indian Railways has withstood the test of time and is basically sound as a government department undertaking. But whether or not it is suitable for a huge commercial undertaking like Indian Railways is highly debatable. The needs of a commercial company are entirely different from those of a government department. A commercial company must display greater flexibility and dynamism. There has to be greater degree of professionalism and accountability. And last but not the least, while seniority cum suitability (not to mention that in the present scheme of things everybody is deemed to be suitable unless proved otherwise) is the norm in government, in a commercial undertaking merit is the only norm.

The structure of Indian Railways, its manning policies and compensation policies must be devised keeping in view the requirements of a huge commercial undertaking.

The Railway Board

It is best to start from the top.

The Railway Board is the highest executive body in Indian Railways. As already mentioned, it is manned by a Chairman and six Members viz. the Financial Commissioner, Member Traffic, Member Civil Engineering, Member Mechanical Engineering, Member Electrical Engineering and Member Staff. Each Member is a functional head of his field. All are highly professional people with many years of service in Indian Railways behind them.

But this composition of the Board is obsolete and not in tune with vastly changed circumstances. Just to cite one example. It was the same composition in 1950–51 when the capital-at-charge was ₹ 827 Crs, revenue ₹ 263 Crs and expenditure ₹ 216 Crs. And it is the same in 2011–12 (except for creation of the post of Member Electrical) when the capital-at-charge is ₹ 1,61,448 Crs. revenue ₹ 106,245 Crs. and expenditure ₹ 99,464 Crs. In 1950–51, Railways moved 93 million tons of freight traffic and 1284 million passengers. In 2011–12, it moved 975.16 million tons of freight and 8224 million passengers. Besides the extraordinary increase in traffic volumes and financial volumes, the challenges of the market have also changed completely. From being a near monopolist, Railways has become only one of the players in the transport market. In addition, Railways is expected to play an unprecedentally larger role in the economic development of the country. Railways must prepare itself for this role.

The composition of the highest executive body must take cognizance of these factors and be moulded accordingly. This calls for change in composition of the Board as well as introduction of more professionalism.

Composition of the Board

The composition of the Railway Board needs to be changed in two ways.

- As argued elsewhere, a post of Member Commercial needs to be created and the existing post of Member Traffic should be designated as Member Operations in charge of operations only.
- Some independent Members need to be inducted into the Board. The Railway Board consists of highly professional persons each of whom would have spent not less than thirty to thirty-five years of service in Indian Railways. There can be no doubt about their professional competence. While there is much to commend for this practice there is also a down side to it. Their life-long service in one single organisation itself works to the disadvantage of the highest executive body of Indian Railways. It is only natural that their perceptions get severely restricted due to long service in one single environment. Their views get firmly heeled, to the extent of dogma. The resistance to change is high. All this gets further accentuated by shortness of tenures. It is precisely because of this reason that many companies resort to lateral entries even at the highest level. This in no way implies that Indian Railways should resort to lateral entries at such a high level. It would be nothing less than catastrophic. It is widely accepted that the railway industry is vastly different from other industries and only a trained and experienced railwayman can succeed in running railways.

But benefit of outsider view and fresh ideas must be availed. Therefore, in order to meet the twin objectives of railway experience plus fresh outsider view, a crucially important element of reform would be to induct experts from other relevant sectors into the Board as Independent Members, such as representatives from industry and finance. Representation from industry could be in the form of Presidents of the three organised associations of industry viz. the Federation of Indian Chamber of Commerce and Industry (FICCI), Chamber of Indian Industries (CII) and Association of Chambers of Commerce (ASSOCHAM). Similarly, representation from the financial sector may be in the form of CMDs of two banks, for example the largest public sector bank the State Bank of India and the largest private sector bank the ICICI Bank. The representation from the financial sector may revolve after say a five-year period or so.

Induction of Independent Members will be of immense value to Railways.

- It will give representation to views of the customers, i.e., the industry.
- It will give an opportunity to benefit from the expertise of the financial sector who have feel for the pulse of the market and the financial sector.
- It will bring in fresh ideas.
- It may, to a great extent, help in resisting external pressures on railways.
- It will multiply the image of railways.

Thus, in place of seven member Board at present, a recast expanded thirteen-Member Board is proposed (Table 11.1).

Needless to say, the designation of the Members will have to change to Directors after corporatisation.

The expanded Board will give it a broad-based profile and provide the much needed commercial outlook, customer orientation and external professional advice from both the industrial and financial sectors. A cross-industry fertilisation of ideas is bound to be of immense benefit to Railways as well as its customers.

It will be noticed that induction of a 'government nominee' on the Board has not been supported in the above scheme, as is customary in the Board of Public Sector Undertakings at present. The presence of a government nominee on the Board, usually of much lower seniority, has not been found of any help. Therefore, their nomination is not really necessary. In fact, the presence of a government nominee on the Board will not be in keeping with the MOU mechanism proposed elsewhere in this book and will impinge upon the freedom of the Board.

Table 11.1: Members of expanded board

Existing Members	*Propsed Members*
Chairman	Chairman
Financial Commissioner	Financial Commissioner
Member Traffic	Member Operations
Memebr Engineering	Member Commercial
Member Mechanical	Memebr Engineering
Member Electrical	Member Mechanical
Memebr Staff	Member Electrical
	Memebr Staff
	Indepnedent Memebr Bank1
	Indepnedent Memebr Bank2
	President FICCI
	President CII
	President ASSOCHAM

Source: Compiled by author

The presence of independent Members is so desirable that they can and should be inducted even now without waiting for corporatisation of Indian Railways.

The existing Board meets quite frequently, as often as weekly, to take care of professional matters. It would neither be practicable nor necessary to have very frequent meetings of the expanded Board. Therefore, there can be a two-tier Board – a functional Board, which may be called the Executive Board consisting of the functional Members and the full expanded Board. The Executive Board may meet as frequently as required. The full Board may meet periodically (at least quarterly as per the requirements of the Companies Act 2013) to take care of important issues. Appropriate structure of powers may be devised indicating the powers of the two types of Boards.

Professionalising the Board

Apart from other examples of ad-hocism in selection for manning some very senior positions in zonal Railways, which are dealt with subsequently, two examples in Railway Board stand out.

- The post of Chairman Railway Board is one prime example. The Chairman Railway Board is the highest ranking railway employee. He presides over one of the largest railway networks in the world. He is in charge of revenue budget of more than ₹ 1,05,000. Crs and capital budget of ₹ 65,000 Crs. or so every year. The capital budget for the year 2013–14 is ₹ 63,363 Crs. He is the leader of 1.3 million staff. Indian Railways has produced some remarkable CRBs in the past. But not always. The question is: whether the existing system of selection can by itself produce a Chairman who is capable enough to lead such an enterprise as Indian Railways, particularly in the context of Indian Railways as a commercial enterprise.

  Normally, not always, the senior-most Member of the Board is elevated as the Chairman of the Board. Sometimes he heads one of the functions also and sometimes he acts as the Chairman only. But in all cases he is a functional specialist who can theoretically be drawn from any of the nine services of Indian Railways, though in the past the CRBs have come from only three departments viz. the Civil Engineering department, the Mechanical Engineering department and the Traffic department. But the job requirements of the Chairman are entirely different from that of a functional specialist. This is discussed further in the 'Railway Executive Service' section.
- Another example of lack of professionalism is the post of Member Staff. At present, the post of Member Staff is manned by an officer of any department. Sometimes by an officer from the Traffic Department, sometimes by an officer from the Civil Engineering Department, sometimes by an officer from the Mechanical Engineering Department, sometimes by an officer from the Electrical Engineering Department and so on. It is no less than the game of musical chairs. There cannot be a better example of casualness. Everybody is supposed to be expert in managing industrial relations, human resources development and staff welfare function of 1.3 million employees. This in spite of there being a professionalised personnel service, the Indian Railway Personnel Service (IRPS), in existence for more than 35 years or so. This hardly seems to be explainable or justifiable. Here, it would not be out of place to mention that an IRPS officer has recently been appointed as Director Personnel in the

Board of Air India. It must be accepted that personnel management is a specialised function and should be handled by specialists. In most of the large companies, the HR function is considered to be a key function.

Railway Executive Service

The senior management posts in Indian Railways can be broadly classified into two types – the technical posts and the general posts. For the purpose of this classification, even posts in the non-technical services such as finance, personnel, traffic etc. may be classified as technical posts. The general posts are also known as non-cadre or ex-cadre posts, i.e., posts outside any particular cadre in Railways. Such posts include those of the Additional Divisional Railway Managers and Divisional Railway Managers in the Divisions, Senior Deputy General Managers, Additional General Managers, General Managers in the zonal railways and the Secretary Railway Board and the Chairman Railway Board in the Ministry of Railways. As per the existing practice, officers of any department can be posted on these posts as long as they are suitable and senior enough. The officers posted in ex-cadre posts, particularly ADRMs and DRMs, return to their parent departments on completion of their assignment.

The ex-cadre posts are also used for what is called 'cadre balancing' meaning thereby that they are used for moving out some persons from the cadre and posted in the ex-cadre posts in order to create vacancies in the cadre for providing promotions in those cadres which are lagging behind other departments in seniority-based promotions. This is a typical example of lack of professionalism and casualness with which the ex-cadre posts are treated. It is the logical consequence of dominance of the seniority syndrome.

This has two harmful effects:

- The fact that the job requirements of the generalist's posts and the technical posts are vastly different is completely overlooked. The job requirement of a technical post is of a technical nature. The officers in the technical stream are expected to be proficient in their own chosen fields, e.g., a Signal engineer should be good in his own field. He need not have more than a nodding acquaintance with finance or labour relations or commercial working of railways. But a DRM's concerns have to be with leadership, commercial matters, finance, labour relations, public relations and other such skills and not so much with the details of technical matters. These are skills which are not taught in colleges (apart from management institutes). They have to be inculcated by consistent and rigorous training, particularly in the context of Railways, and updated from time to time. It is wasteful to train a person in these skills and by the time he gets familiar with using it, he reverts to his parent department. Actually, such training is not imparted even at present. Far from it. The officers posted as Additional Divisional Railway Managers, Divisional Railway Managers are left to fend for themselves as best as they can. Therefore, more often than not they work according to their common sense or rather sixth sense on suddenly being posted to the ex-cadre posts. No wonder quite a few of them do flounder.

- It has also been observed that the officers posted to these ex-cadre posts bring with them a bias for their cadre. Indian Railway officers have often been criticised for too strong departmental affiliations to the extent that it influences their decisions. But it would not be fair to place the entire blame on them. It is only natural human behaviour to have a soft corner for past associations and for the department to which they will go back in the near future. The blame should be put squarely on the practice which requires the officers to revert to the parent cadre after completion of a short stint in the ex-cadre posts.

The only effective way of tackling the above problems would be to create a separate Indian Railway Executive Service (IRES) from among serving railway officers of sufficient seniority. It is only the officers of IRES who should be posted on the generalists' posts. And once the officers are selected for these posts, they should be required to continue in and look for career progression in the general posts only. Their relationship with their parent departments should be completely severed. It is worth mentioning that Tatas, one of the foremost and professionally managed companies, have their own management cadre called Tata Administrative Service.

The main aim of this suggestion is to:

- Reduce departmental affiliations in ex-cadre posts.
- Professionalise these posts by imparting in such selected persons, specialised training in managerial skills required for managing Railways as a commercial enterprise.
- Having created such specialised persons, retain them for the benefit of the organisation.

The broad contours of such a scheme could be as follows:

- The cadre of IRES should be created out of serving railway officers only and not be recruited afresh through Union Public Service Commission like other railway services or other services of the government. It is important that the officers inducted into IRES should be of middle management level having sufficient railway background otherwise it will become only another administrative service defeating the very purpose of having a set of officers who are well versed in railway matters as well as equipped with managerial skills. Direct recruitment to IRES will be a case of the cure being worse than the disease.
- The induction into IRES should be at the level of Additional Divisional Railway Managers.
- Officers who have put in a certain length of service, say twelve to fifteen years or so, in any department, should be given an option to join the cadre of IRES.
- The seniority of IRES officers should be on an all-India basis.
- Therefore, the selection to the entry grade should be done under the aegis of the Railway Board, by a committee consisting of Heads of Departments of Personnel, Finance and Commercial departments from three different zonal railways to ensure impartiality. Membership of the Selection Committee should be restricted to Finance and Commercial departments besides that of the Personnel department in order to emphasise the role of commerce and finance in their future career.
- After selection they should be trained in appropriate skills such as railway finance, labour laws, commercial aspect of railway working, leadership, interpersonal skills and communication skills before posting.
- Once they join the cadre of IRES they should not go back to their parent departments.
- After recruitment and before promotion to each higher grade, there should be a process of selection and elimination at every stage so that only the very best rise to become General Managers and the Chairman Railway Board. Needless to say, this process would give more weightage to merit than seniority.
- The selection for the posts of General Managers and the Chairman Railway Board should be done by the Public Enterprises Selection

Board/Union Public Service Commission to remove any hint of bias or favouritism.

- Any Divisional Railway Manager, irrespective of seniority should be eligible to apply for the post of General Manager and any General Manager should be eligible to apply for the post of the Chairman Railway Board. However, it has been suggested elsewhere that the tenure of CRB should be at least five years and that of the General Manager should be at least three years. This aspect may have to be kept in mind while deciding the eligibility criteria for these posts.
- Initially, it would not be possible to frame an entire cadre only through direct induction of new entrants to IRES, as direct entry to IRES is proposed at the level of Additional Railway Managers only. Therefore, it will be necessary to form the cadre by extending the option to join IRES to those holding ex-cadre posts at the time of implementation of the scheme, as was done at the time of formation of Indian Railway Personnel Service in the 1970s.
- Until IRES is formed, the posts of General Managers should be filled up by UPSC/PSEB by calling for options from eligible (by way of age) Heads of Department and DRMs of all zonal Railways. And the posts of DRMs may be continued to be filled up as at present to the extent that direct entry ADRMs with sufficient seniority and experience as ADRMs are not available.
- The selection for the posts of General Manager and the Chairman Railway Board has been discussed above. A similar approach needs to be followed in the case of posts of other Members of the Railway Board viz. those of the Financial Commissioner, Member Operations, Member Commercial, Member Engineering, Member Mechanical, Member Electrical, Member Signal and Telecommunications and Member Staff. Their selection should also be made by the Public Enterprises Selection Board/Union Public Service Commission. And any officer of the concerned department who is in the grade immediately below that of the Member should be eligible to apply for it. This would ensure giving preference to merit over seniority.

In a government type of set-up seniority is sacrosanct. However, it is not so in a business environment. In a competitive business environment, rules of the game must change. Seniority must give way to merit. It will be observed that in all the suggestions above merit and youth are proposed to be given preference over seniority.

With 17 zones (including Kolkata Metro) each having a General Manager, at least one Additional General Manager and a Senior Deputy General Manager, 68 Divisions having one Divisional Railway Manager and at least one Additional Divisional Railway Manager (some divisions have as many as three Additional Divisional Railway Managers) it will not be too difficult to form a complete cadre of railway managers having an appropriate channel of promotion.

Special class railway apprentice

This is an anachronism that exists from the days of British rule.

At present, mechanical engineers in railways are recruited in two ways – as Special Class Railway Apprentices and as Graduate Engineers. Both the recruitments are made through competitive examination conducted by Union Public Service Commission (UPSC) of India but with different selection criteria.

The eligibility for recruitment as Special Class Railway Apprentice (SCRAs) is only a pass in Class 12, although even graduates and post-graduates are known to appear for this examination. After selection, the SCRAs are taught and trained by railway mechanical engineers for a period of four years in Indian Railway Institute for Electrical and Mechanical Engineers at Jamalpur in Bihar. After completion of that training, they join the Probationary Officers of other branches of Railways such as Civil Engineering, Electrical Engineering, Signal & Telecommunications Engineering, Stores, Finance, Traffic and Personnel departments as also graduate Mechanical Engineers recruited through competitive examinations conducted by the Union Public Service Commission. After the completion of probationary period of two years, the SCRAs are posted as Class 1 officers like directly recruited officers of other departments.

The institute is not authorised to award an engineering degree. Therefore, the Apprentices are encouraged to acquire an engineering degree through correspondence courses. The institute has produced some excellent mechanical engineers in the past who have acquitted themselves well, both within the railways as well as outside the railways.

As mentioned above, the second method of recruitment of mechanical engineers in railways is through the competitive examination conducted by the Union Public Service Commission of India from graduate engineers as in the case of engineers of other departments.

Thus, the Mechanical Engineering department is the only department in railways in which engineers are recruited in two ways. Existence of officers in the same department, occupying the same level of posts but recruited in two different ways has, understandably, led to strong group affiliations resulting into undercurrent of simmering discontent and conflict among the two sets of officers.

It is now time to consider whether the practice of recruiting officers in two ways in the same department should continue at the cost of internal cohesion.

The need for recruitment to SCRA in the British days arose because of three reasons – shortage of graduate mechanical engineers, technology for steam engine and other kinds of rolling stock being simple and thirdly the senior positions in the mechanical engineering department was scarcely open to Indian engineers.

Now that graduate mechanical engineers are available in plenty, there does not appear to be any rationale for continuing with this anachronistic practice anymore at the cost of cohesion in the department.

Professionalising the non-technical functions

There are nine departments in railways to which recruitments are made through the UPSC out of which Finance, Traffic and Personnel are considered as non-technical departments. In the case of all other departments only professionally qualified candidates are eligible for selection. But in the case of Finance, Traffic and Personnel departments graduates of any discipline, such as Engineering, Medical, Pure Sciences, History, Political Science, Economics, Philosophy, Commerce, English Literature, Hindi, Urdu, Persian, Sanskrit and what have you, are eligible to apply and get selected.

After selection the officers of the non-technical departments are put through a two-year class room training in railway training institutes and on-job training programme on different railways, workshops and production units like officers of other departments (except for the Medical department). During this period, the trainees are expected to learn not only the theoretical aspects of their chosen profession, which would decidedly be new to them, but also Indian Railways in general and the rules and procedures applicable to their discipline in depth. The field of training is vast. Clearly, it would be naïve to expect these officers to have more than nodding acquaintance with any of these areas at the end of the decidedly rigorous training period including a number of examinations.

It needs to be kept in mind that this is the age of specialisation. And professionally qualified people are now available in diverse fields in abundance. There is no reason why if entry to engineering services can be restricted to qualified engineers, entry to Finance, Commercial, Personnel and Stores departments should not be restricted to persons qualified in relevant disciplines.

The approach towards manning different functions in railways must change in keeping with times. At the entry level itself, railways should get as much professionally qualified persons as possible. Their college level professional education may then need only to be supplemented with knowledge and skills specifically required for railways. This is bound to improve the professional competence of those officers.

For example,

- The entry to the Finance department may be restricted to graduates in Commerce, Economics, MBA (Finance), Chartered Accountants, Chartered Financial Analysts and Cost Accountants.
- Entry to the Commercial department may be restricted to graduates in Commerce, Economics, MBA (Finance), MBA (Marketing and Sales).
- Entry to the Personnel department should be restricted to persons qualified in Human Resource Management or Industrial Relations.
- Entry to the Stores department may be restricted to persons qualified in Supply Chain Management or Logistics Management.
- At present, it is not possible to adopt the same principle in respect of the Operating branch of the Traffic department as no professional qualification exists which may be especially suitable for the Operating department. In their case, therefore, recruitment may be restricted to MBAs in any specialisation preferably MBAs in Marketing, Finance, Human Resource Management and so on.

It is time that Indian railways adopt a more professional approach. Instead of officers we need to have professionals.

Tenures

Indian Railways is a large and complex organisation playing a crucial role in the economic activity of the country. It would not be an exaggeration to say that it is a state within state. Such an organisation requires a reasonable tenure for persons at the helm of affairs. What exists in actual practice is exactly to the contrary. The tenure of its senior-most officers viz. the Chairman and Members of the Railway Board varies from four months to two years at the maximum. There is more stability of tenure in the case of General Managers. Although orders exist regarding a minimum tenure of two years, it is observed more in violation than in its compliance. It is, therefore, not surprising that most of such officers treat their posting as 'time pass' or just maintaining the *status quo* – let things continue as they are. It is unfair to expect them to take any initiative which they may not be able see through. Unless this short-sighted practice is done away with, it is futile to expect any change in the fortune of Indian Railways. Any number of experts and Committees have strongly advised against this pernicious practice and suggested a minimum tenure of five years.

It is suggested that the minimum tenure of the CRB and Members of the Board should be five years and that of the General Manager of a Railway should be three years, longer the better. The tenure of five years should be achieved not by extending the service beyond the prescribed age of superannuation but by picking the Chairman and the Members before they reach the age of fifty five. This will not only give a reasonable period of time to the incumbents to put their ideas into practice, it will ensure younger and more agile minds to take charge of affairs.

The suggestion of picking the Chairman of the Railway Board from the proposed management service only is also bound to raise hackles in most corners. But a clear distinction between the job requirement of a Chairman and other Members needs to be accepted.

The above measures will, no doubt, lead to supersession, which actually is the intention of the proposed scheme. And it is bound to cause extreme dissatisfactions in a system long accustomed to the rule of seniority. But this dissatisfaction will be a temporary phenomenon. It would be just a matter of time before people come to accept supersession as normal as is the case in private sector. If an organisation has to compete with the dynamism and agility of the private sector it must adopt some of the norms and practices of the private sector.

12

Incentive Scheme

Management theorists say that though reward and punishment should go hand in hand, reward is a better instrument than punishment to spur performance. And for reward to act as a good motivation there should be proper relationship between reward and performance – the type of reward and the type of performance, quantum of reward, timing of the reward, a direct and visible relationship between reward and performance and so on. It is only when these elements exist that reward can act as an incentive to perform.

An incentive scheme in Railways does exist in the form of Productivity Linked Bonus. But it has singularly failed to act as an incentive scheme. It has become a purely employee welfare scheme.

The Government of India enacted the Payment of Bonus Act 1965 for its employees. According to this Act, bonus was payable to certain categories of industrial workers under the government. But as per Section 32(iv), this Act was not applicable to

> employees employed by an establishment engaged in any industry carried on by or under the authority of any department of the Central Government or State Government or local authority.

Thus, the Bonus Act was not applicable to many government organisations such as the Postal department, Defence, Employee State Insurance Scheme, Railways etc. In order to remove these lacunae, the government permitted those departments to evolve their own Bonus schemes linked to productivity.

Productivity Linked Bonus Scheme

Railways were the first to develop and implement the Productivity Linked Bonus Scheme. It came into force from the year 1979–80. The broad features of the scheme are as follows:

(a) Productivity is calculated by dividing output by input. Output is the sum total of freight tonne km and passenger km converted to tonne km according to certain weightages. Input is the number of non-gazetted employees adjusted by increase/decrease in wagon capacity and passenger coach capacity during the year.
(b) The ratio of the output to the input is the productivity index for the year.
(c) If the productivity index falls below 90, no bonus is payable.
(d) Based on the productivity index for the year, the number of days for payment of Bonus is sanctioned with the approval of the government.
(e) The above calculations for determining the number of days is done at an all-India level, i.e., the figures of output, input etc. are taken for Indian Railways as a whole.
(f) Bonus is paid to all non-Gazetted Railway employees only.
(g) Although Bonus is payable to all non-gazetted employees, the amount per day is calculated at the maximum salary of ₹ 3,500 per month.

The following amounts ware paid as bonus to railway employees since 2001–02 (Table 12.1).

Table 12.1: Bonus since 2001–02 (₹ Crs.)

Year	*Days*	*Amount*
2001–02	59	484.9
2002–03	59	484.9
2003–04	59	483.6
2004–05	59	484.9
2005–06	65	534.2
2006–07	70	575.3
2007–08	73	839.9
2008–09	75	863.0
2009–10	77	886.0
2010–11	78	897.5
2011–12	78	935.71

Source: Compiled by author

The PLB scheme of Railways suffers from a number of flaws.

- The output for the purpose of the PLB scheme is taken in physical terms only viz. traffic units. It does not take into account financial health of the organisation. It is often argued that this is quite logical. After all, it is only the physical factors that can be controlled by railway employees. The financial results mostly depend on factors such as railway tariffs, cost of fuel, salaries and wages which are as per government rules and outside the control of railway employees. Therefore, the only course open is to relate productivity to physical output alone.

  The above statement is only partly true. While the other factors enumerated above may be outside the control of Railways, the number of employees is certainly within the control of Railways.

  Further, the PLB scheme as it exists has an inherent risk. If bonus is related to physical output alone, a situation may arise where even if Railways is in loss, bonus will still have to be paid. This is a sure recipe for financial disaster and bankruptcy.

  It is actually happening. As shown in Table 12.2, in the year 2011–12 Bonus was paid in CR, ER, NR, NER,NFR, SR and SWR Railways though they had negative Net Revenues. The highest bonus of ₹ 115.36 Crs was paid by NR which had negative Net Revenue of ₹ 2196.68 Crs.

Table 12.2: Bonus and Net Revenue in 2011–12 (₹ Crs)

	Net Rev	*Bonus*
CR	-432.55	82.02
ER	-3331.72	78.39
ECR	18.21	61.22
ECoR	4620.88	31.49
NR	-2196.68	115.36
NCR	3536.60	54.27
NER	-1911.06	41.54
NFR	-1195.95	52.01
NWR	122.94	40.88

Contd.

Contd.

	Net Rev	*Bonus*
SR	-1219.76	67.64
SCR	1436.15	67.71
SER	2254.78	61.17
SECR	2970.38	31.20
SWR	-205.03	23.09
WR	472.72	80.52
WCR	2029.77	44.48
Total		933.28

Note: The above figures of Net Revenue and PLB are slightly different from actual total figures of IR as some organisations such as Railway Board, RDSO, Training Institutes, Metro Railways have been left out. In any case, their figures are too small to make any difference to our analysis.
Source: Compiled by author

The starkness of the picture becomes much clearer in the form of a graph (Chart 12.1).

Chart 12.1: Net Revenue & PLB

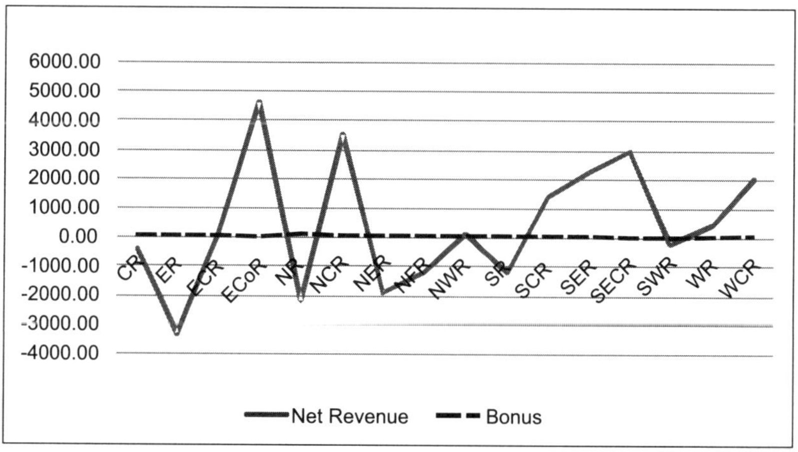

The only saving grace so far has been that while seven out of sixteen zonal railways had negative Net Revenue, Indian Railways as a whole had positive Net Revenue.

Extrapolating the picture a little further, it is not difficult to imagine a situation where bonus will have to be paid even if the Net Revenue of Indian Railways as a whole is negative. This, to say the least, is nothing short of scandalous.

The above example clearly brings out the fundamental deficiency of the scheme.

This flaw was commented upon by the Sixth Central Pay Commission (1998) also. In their Report the Commission had recommended that the PLB formulae should be modified in a way where bonus has a direct nexus with the increased profitability/ productivity under well-defined financial parameters. The Commission further said that in the case of railway's PLB, a new formula should be devised which should be based on financial parameters and where profit is computed as per the established principles of commercial accounting with appropriate adjustments for increases in the impact of the capital investment, element of subsidy, etc.

Needless to say, this has not yet been done in spite of the lapse of fifteen years.

The above situation has arisen purely because the PLB scheme is based on physical parameters alone.

It must be accepted by all, including the Trade Unions, that in a situation where an organisation is in financial crisis, employees of the organisation cannot and should not remain completely indifferent to and in isolation of its financial health.

- Another important flaw is that PLB is calculated at a macro level.

Bonus is expected to act as an incentive scheme. And for an incentive scheme to act as such in an effective manner, the relationship between reward and performance should be as direct and visible as possible so that the recipient is able to relate his reward to his effort. In this respect, the PLB scheme is structurally defective. At present, the entitlement of number of days for Bonus is calculated at the all-railway level. The all-India performance of railways is too distant from the beneficiaries of the Bonus. It is not possible for any employee to relate his performance to the reward he receives. Thus, for a railway employee who receives the Bonus, it is just a windfall income.

The PLB scheme can be likened to the Group Incentive Scheme in railway workshops. The Group Incentive Scheme is applicable in cases where it is not possible to link output to the performance of a single individual but it is possible to link it with the performance of a group of individuals. But Group Incentive Scheme is only the second best option and is applied only where the individual incentive scheme cannot be applied. Therefore, even in the Group Incentive Scheme, the effort is to have as small a group as possible so as to link reward as closely as possible to performance. Same is the case with PLB. The only difference is that in case of PLB, the Group i.e. the entire Indian Railways, is too large to have any impact.

Therefore, a method which reduces the size of the Group would be preferable. Smaller the Group, better it is.

- The existing PLB scheme is applicable to the non-gazetted staff only. This feature has been borrowed from the Bonus Act 1965. Excluding other than the non-gazetted staff, i.e., the management cadre, does not stand to reason. It conveys the impression that the managers either do not play any role in the process of production or that they do not need any incentive. Both the impressions are unsustainable. No such presumptions are made in the private sector which are universally lauded for their productive efficiency.

  Actually these myths have been given a go by even in the government sector. Arising from the recommendations of the Sixth Pay Commissioning the Government announced implementation of a Performance Related Incentive Scheme (PRIS) for Central Government Employees in March 2011, according to which even such senior officers as Secretaries of the Government of India become entitled to incentives.

  Thus, there is no reason as to why the Bonus Scheme in Railways should not be extended to the highest level of management including the Chairman Railway Board.

- Further, the highest amount of bonus is currently calculated at the maximum basic salary of ₹ 3,500 per month. This works out to about ₹ 11,000 per year or ₹ 917 per month. With the current level of prices it is too small to act as an incentive. To make it attractive the bonus amount should be related to the actual basic pay drawn by an employee.

The suggestions regarding – (i) extending the Incentive scheme to all categories of employees and (ii) relating it to actual basic salary drawn by an employee might appear to lead to an increase in expenditure on total bonus payment of Indian Railways.

But as will become clear from the alternative incentive scheme proposed below, this need not necessarily be so. And if it does happen, it would be a most welcome situation as it would imply a very substantial all-round improvement in physical as well as financial performance of Railways. The basis of saying so will become clearer after the proposed scheme is explained.

The alternative Incentive Scheme proposed below tries to remove the shortcomings of the existing scheme by:

- Linking bonus to both physical and financial performance.
- Bringing input and output as close as possible to the beneficiaries.
- Extending the scheme to all employees including the management.
- Increasing the salary level for calculating bonus.

Alternative Incentive Scheme

There is one fundamental difference between emoluments in the private sector and those in the government sector. Usually the emoluments in the private sector consist of two parts – a fixed part and a variable part. While the fixed part of emolument, as the name indicates is fixed which the employee is sure to get, the variable part is linked to performance of the employee. The variable part actually acts as the incentive to perform. In addition, Bonus may also be paid depending upon the financial performance of the company as a whole. That is one of the main reasons why the private sector scores over the government sector by miles in respect of productive efficiency.

It would be useful to borrow some part of this idea from the private sector. While at present, it is not possible to have the two part concept in respect of salaries, it could be gainfully employed in the Incentive Scheme proposed below as successor to the Productivity Linked Bonus scheme.

An important feature of the existing PLB scheme is that the Bonus is calculated for IR as a whole. In the method proposed below, the incentive is to be calculated for each zonal railway separately.

Based on the above two elements the proposed incentive methodology is explained step-wise.

- Calculate the incentive number of days for each zonal railway separately, based on physical input and output as under the existing PLB scheme. Some modification to the existing methodology for giving weightage to increase in total wagon capacity and seating capacity of coaches on the zonal railway during the year may be called for. Some method may also have to be devised to take into account other items of capital input such as investment on signalling etc.
- Assume a certain percentage, say 50 per cent, of it as a fixed component and the balance 50 per cent as the variable component.
- The variable component should be linked to financial performance of the concerned zonal railways in terms of increase in Net Revenue or reduction in losses over that of the previous year.

  It needs to be emphasised that what is being talked about is not the absolute value of the Net Revenue – whether positive or negative. It is the improvement element over the previous year which is relevant – increase in positive value or decrease in negative value.

  Thus, the variable component of incentive will become payable even on zonal railways which have negative Net Revenue if the negative Net Revenue on those railways has come down compared to the previous year. And conversely the variable component of incentive will not become payable on such zonal railways which do have a positive Net Revenue but the Net Revenue has either remained constant or reduced as compared to the previous year.

  Thus, it is the improvement element in financial terms which represents efforts made to increase revenues and/or cut costs, which is sought to be rewarded. Such emphasis on improving the Net Revenue of the railway will have immense impact on inculcating commercial culture in the organisation.
- Every percentage increase in Net Revenue or decrease in losses would lead to a percentage increase/decrease in variable part of the bonus. For example, it might be decided that every 10 per cent increase in Net Revenue or every 10 per cent reduction in losses would lead to earning 10 per cent of the variable incentive days such that full variable incentive days are earned when Net Revenue increases or losses are reduced by 100 per cent over the previous year. If there is no increase in Net Revenue or reduction in losses no variable incentive is earned.

  A sample calculation based on Net Revenue figures for 2010–11 and 2011–12 is shown in Table 12.3 in order to clarify the concept.

Table 12.3: Net Revenue for PLB calculation (₹ Crs)

Rly	*Net Rev. 2010–11*	*Net Rev. 2011–12*	*Difference*	*Improvement*	*% Imp*
CR	-481	-432.55	48.45	48.45	10
ER	-2952	-3331.7	-379.72	0	0
NR	-1516	-2196.7	-680.68	0	0
NER	-1670	-1911.1	-241.08	0	0
NFR	-1133	-1196	-62.95	0	0
SR	-1620	-1219.8	400.24	400.24	25
SCR	1257	1436.15	179.15	179.15	14
SER	2595	2254.78	-340.22	0	0
WR	241	472.72	231.72	231.72	96
ECR	-306	18.21	324.21	324.21	106
ECoR	5105	4620.8	-484.2	0	0
NCR	3021	3536.9	515.9	515.9	17
NWR	-121	122.94	243.94	243.94	202
SECR	2448	2970.38	522.38	522.38	21
SWR	97	-205.03	-302.03	0	0
WCR	1458	2029.77	571.77	571.77	39

Source: Compiled by author

Please note that what is being calculated is not whether the Net Revenue is positive or negative, but whether there is an 'improvement'. If the negative Net Revenue in the current year is less than the negative Net Revenue in the previous year, then it is an improvement as in the case of Central Railway or Southern Railway above. Hence, these railways will be entitled to variable incentive days. On the other hand, even if the Net Revenue remains positive during both the years but it goes down compared to the previous year as in the case of East Coast Railway and South East Railway, the improvement is nil. Hence, they would not be entitled to the variable incentive days.

The last column shows the percentage entitlement of variable incentive days, after ignoring the negative signs (which have arisen because of negative Net Revenue in the base year). Of course, the percentage entitlement cannot be more than 100 per cent.

Thus, even loss making railways become entitled to variable incentive days if they succeed in reducing their losses. Financial improvement over the previous year is the crux for the entitlement of variable incentive.

A big advantage of the proposed methodology is that both the physical performance and financial performance are given due weightage. The fixed element gives weightage to physical performance and the variable element gives weightage to financial performance.

- The next problem with the existing PLB scheme is its calculation at a macro level such that there is no direct and visible relationship between reward and effort. Hence, it is incapable of making any impact. In the method proposed above, the calculation is done for each zonal railway separately. Thus, the size of the group gets considerably reduced and a closer, more direct and visible relationship between reward and effort is established. Such a calculation is even now possible because both the physical data and the financial data for each zonal railway are already separately available.

  But even the proposed method is not quite satisfactory. It is still quite macro, though much less than the existing one. It has been suggested elsewhere in this book that each railway Division should ultimately be made a business unit. When that happens, the incentives according to the proposed method can be calculated for each Division. This will further reduce the size of the group and establish a closer relationship between reward and effort.

  Thus, the proposed method is vastly better than the existing method as the reward is more directly, visibly and closely related to performance as compared to the existing scheme.

- At present, all non-gazetted employees are covered by the PLB scheme including those in production units, construction organisations, training institutes, RDSO and so forth. The employees of these organisations no doubt do contribute to the working of railways, but indirectly. They are in no way related with the performance of open line railway. They should, therefore, be taken out of this calculation. And only the open line staff should be considered as the input (i.e. the denominator) in the formulae for calculating the number of days for incentive entitlement. This in no way implies that they should not be given any incentive payment. Only that their bonus formulae should be related to the type of work that they do.

For example, the incentives for employees of construction organisation could be related to the timely completion of projects, maintaining tight control on actual cost vis-a-vis estimated cost etc. This will bring greater discipline in framing of estimates and execution of projects both with respect to time as well as cost.

- Bonus should be paid to all categories of employees including the Chairman Railway Board. If that happens it is natural to expect that governed by human nature, the powers in railways will pay more attention to physical as well as financial performance of railways – increasing revenues and cutting costs.
- The maximum amount of bonus should not be restricted to the salary level of ₹ 3,500. It should be related to the actual basic salary drawn by an employee or to the minimum basic salary of the scale of pay to which the employee belongs.

As mentioned earlier, the proposed scheme gives the impression that extending the Incentive Scheme to all categories of employees and calculating incentives with reference to the actual salary drawn or to the minimum basic salary may lead to increase in total incentive payment as compared to the payment under the existing method. But this need not necessarily be so. Because it will be seen that in the proposed method the variable incentive is payable not in all railways but only in railways which show financial improvement over the previous year. It is quite possible that not all zonal railways would show such improvement and would, therefore, not be eligible for variable incentive days. Thus, the increase in incentive in one railway may get set off by reduction in another railway. And if there is actually an overall increase, it should be welcomed as it would reflect very substantial improvement in financial performance of many railways over the previous year.

As regards relating per day incentive amount to actual basic salary of the employee as against the present practice of restricting it to the salary level of ₹ 3500 per month is concerned, it can only be said that an incentive should not just be a token amount. It should be respectable enough to effectively act as an incentive. The resultant improvement in employee morale and consequent improvement in productivity, it is believed, will more than offset any increase in expenditure.

The above method does not deal with employees of such organisations as Railway Board, Research Design and Standards Organisation, Training institutes etc as they are basically cost centres. The concept of Net Revenue is not applicable in their case. But all railways do benefit from their work. Therefore, in the case of these organisations the above method may have to be applied by taking Indian Railways as one unit or on the basis of average of all railways.

It is inevitable that in the proposed method, there would be difference between incentives received by employees of different railways although they may be in the same category and in the same scale of pay doing the same work. This is not entirely undesirable from the point of view of productivity. In fact, this is exactly as it should be and this is what the proposed method tries to do.

It is well realised that no scheme can be successful without the full support of organised labour. It would, therefore, be of crucial importance to first bring the Trade Unions on board. It is not going to be easy, but not impossible. It has to be a part of the reform process. Organised labour has to realise that in a commercial environment they have to share the financial prosperity as well as the adversity of the organisation.

13

The Core and Non-core Debate

There is a strong body of opinion that a business concern must identify its core area of activity and concentrate on the core area rather than waste its time and resources on activities that can be easily outsourced. Recalling the Ricardo principle – if country A can produce apples cheaper than country B and country B can produce oranges more cheaply, it is better that A produces apples and B produces oranges and they exchange, rather than both producing apples and oranges more expensively. It does make a lot of sense.

Translated into terms of companies, it may be said that a company should as far as possible stick to its areas of core competence and hive off its other activities. This will enable it to produce more efficiently and hence at lower costs. Its non-core activities can be carried out by some other companies for which those activities may form activities of their core competence. In this way, the economy benefits and the consumer gets the goods and services at the lowest cost. Based on this argument, experts have been suggesting that Indian Railways should also stick to its core business of transportation and shed off its other activities.

But the real world is not as simple as the Ricardian world.

First of all it is necessary to be clear about the concept of 'core competence' itself. What actually does core competence mean? Can a company have more than one area of core competence?

What is the core competence area for say Godrej – furniture or locks or refrigerators or real estate? What is the core competence area for Mahindra and Mahindra – tractors, motor vehicles or software? What is the core competence area for Tata – steel, motor vehicles, consultancy, salt, chemicals, airlines, insurance or Starbucks coffee just to name a few? What is the core competence area for Wipro – soap or oil or software? Similarly, for Reliance Industries – is it petroleum or textile or vegetables or malls or selling chicken etc.? The list is endless not only in India but throughout the world. Can we say that these leaders of business and industry do not know the fundamentals of business?

The principle which then emerges is – If you can make money by selling ice creams: Why not? This turns expert wisdom on its head.

The concept which can be rationally justified is that an activity which increases revenue and/or reduces cost thereby increasing profit is an activity fit for being taken up by a commercial concern. The operating word is 'increasing profit'. It would not be very correct to classify an activity as core or non-core for deciding whether to shed off or not. A better classification would be 'profitable' or 'non-profitable'. We may add 'convenience' also to the list.

Let us now examine the business of Indian Railways.

In case of railways, transportation of goods and passengers is the core activity. All other activities may strictly be classified as non-core activities. Various experts have, therefore, suggested hiving off or rather privatising a number of activities – ranging from production units, hospitals, schools, colony maintenance, catering, linen supply in coaches, repair and maintenance facilities, issuing of passenger tickets, booking of freight consignments etc.

Before examining the recommendations, it is first necessary to discuss some general considerations affecting the concept of core and non-core itself.

In many cases there could be some activities which are totally unrelated, for example watch and ward. But in case of most large-scale economic entities a straightaway black and white classification into core and non-core activities is misleading. There is a grey area or intermediate zone which we may call semi-core activities. These are activities which are not strictly core but which are integral to the core to make it function economically or smoothly. Whether such non-core or semi-core activities should be hived off will depend on a number of considerations.

- One important consideration is the size of the main activity and the relative size of the non-core activity. For example, a trucker having only a couple of trucks may not find it advantageous to develop in-house repair and maintenance facility. But a trucker owning a large fleet of trucks would definitely find it not only advantageous but essential to have his own in-house repair shop. The Delhi Transport Corporation, one of the largest bus transportation companies in the world, has its own repair and maintenance facility.

- Cost is another consideration. It may be cheaper to have an in-house facility than to outsource the activity.
- If repair work is proposed to be hived off, it may even be difficult to define and determine all items of work involved, in order to obtain quotable cost of a work. For example, although repair and maintenance of rolling stock can be said to be a non-core activity, it would be virtually impossible to define and concretise all aspects of repair and maintenance work to enable the tenderer to quote his rates. It would also lead to endless disputes later on as happened in British Rail. Some smaller railways have got around this problem by off-loading the repair and maintenance of locomotives without specifying the item of work to be done but specifying an 'up time' of the locos. This has its own complications – dry lease versus wet lease, costs, problems arising at the time of termination of existing contract and fixing of new contract etc.
- Convenience and ease of availability are other important considerations.

Thus, there are no straight answers to this question. It cannot be straightaway said whether an activity is core or non-core and should or should not be shed off. There is need to avoid rhetoric and doctrinaire approach. Each and every case should to be decided on merit.

Four activities of Indian Railways are generally recommended by experts as fit candidates for hiving off or privatisation – production units, health, education and retiring rooms, not taking into account such minor activities as colony maintenance, supply of linen in coaches. Supply of linen in coaches is a fully off-line non-core activity and is in most cases already being executed through contract. Privatising of colony maintenance is a touchy issue and has its own problems. It is not being discussed here. Production units are discussed separately in Chapter 14. The other three are discussed below.

Health services

Indian Railways has a very good network of medical facilities for its personnel. It is, perhaps, next only to the Army hospitals. Its reach is far and wide. The medical department in Indian Railways is headed by Director General Health Services in the Railway Board reporting to Member Staff. In addition to a main hospital in each zonal railway and large size hospitals in Divisional Headquarters, there are a large number of smaller hospitals and Health Units/

Dispensaries in almost all mid-size railway colonies. For remote colonies and stations, medical facilities are provided through travelling doctors.

It is little realised that railway hospitals offer one of the best treatments in the country at least cost – least cost is important. The railway hospital in Chennai was the first in India to conduct open heart surgery and is still considered by many to be at least as good as most of the well-known private hospitals, shorn of the five star frills. Same applies to BR Singh Hospital in Kolkata for orthopaedic treatment. In fact, a large number of non-railway persons prefer treatment in railway hospitals due to the competence, care and facilities in railway hospitals compared to government hospitals and cost compared to private hospitals. During the year 2012–13, Indian Railways spent ₹ 1581.20 Crs. on medical facilities in railways which works out to about ₹ 1760 per person per annum (considering a family size of five for serving employees and two for retired employees). This is perhaps the cheapest medical facility of reasonable quality anywhere in the country, except the government hospitals where the quality of medical care is always suspect, barring the All Indian Institute of Medical Sciences at Delhi. It is in no way the case that this meagre amount on health care of railway employees is adequate. In fact, it is quite the contrary. Much more needs to be spent on health care of the employees to bring it even up to a satisfactory level. However, what is being discussed is whether hiving it off would be better – either as a separate organisation still within the railway umbrella or privatising it altogether. As is the experience with private hospitals in India, privatising railway hospitals, i.e., selling it off to a private medical chain, cannot be considered a rational option. It is not difficult to imagine the astronomical cost of medical care for 1.3 million railway employees and about half the number of railway pensioners and their family Members which the railways will have to bear in case of privatisation of railways' health services. This option is just not worth considering.

The next option is to carve it out as a separate organisation within Railways. This option does not appear to confer any tangible advantage either, unless it is opened up to non-railway persons in a big way and required to run at profit or at least meet its costs. It has been suggested by some experts that railway hospitals should be commercialised and made a source of profit. If that happens the quality of service to railwaymen is bound to get severely compromised, which will defeat the very purpose of having a railway medical facility. There will remain little difference between privatisation of railway hospitals and converting it into a separate organisation under the umbrella of Railways with a profit motive. Health care should never be made a source of profit as is the case with private hospitals.

It is not quite clear as to why railway medical service is recommended for being shed off – would it provide better service or be any cheaper? No doubt it would be possible to provide better medical facilities after privatisation. But it will certainly not be cheap. And better facilities can be provided even in railway hospitals with more infusion of funds.

Based on the logic of shedding off medical service in railways, could there be a similar case for shedding off medical services in the Indian Army? On the other hand, the Indian Army has gone a step further and has set up Army Medical Colleges of its own.

Shedding off railway medical facility can in no way be rationally justified. On the contrary, there is a strong case for its strengthening.

Education facilities

Indian Railways run a number of schools in railway colonies. This practice started long time back in residential colonies where either no schools existed or those which existed were of poor standard.

That is not the case anymore. Now Kendriya Vidyalays have come up at a number of places and are still expanding. A number of other schools have also come up at most of the places where railway colonies are situated. Where Kendriya Vidyalays do not exist at present the Kendriya Vidyalay Sangthan can be persuaded to set up such schools in railway colonies for which Railways may provide infrastructure facilities as may be required. This would not only be cheaper for railways, it will also put education of railway children in more professional hands.

In view of the above, the practice of having railway schools can be given up.

Retiring rooms

Some activities can not only be meaningfully shed off but also made a source of profit. A prime example is railway retiring rooms. There are retiring rooms at most of the important railway stations for the use of railway passengers on payment of nominal charges. The charges are low and so is the quality of service.

A proper approach would be to hand over all the retiring rooms to the Indian Railway Catering and Tourism Corporation (IRCTC), a company under the Ministry of Railways. IRCTC could upgrade them as required, add more retiring rooms where they already exist or set up new ones where they do not exist and run them as regular budget hotels located in railway premises. IRCTC is already in the hospitality business through catering operations and budget hotels at a few stations. With perennial shortage of budget hotels not only in big cities but even in the so-called Tier 2 and Tier 3 cities, a hotels division of IRCTC could be a very lucrative business indeed. The untapped market is vast.

Thus, while shedding off health service is totally unadvisable, shedding off education facility to Kendriya Vidyalay Sangthan and retiring rooms to IRCTC is much desirable.

14

Production Units

Indian Railways is a fully vertically integrated system. It not only owns and maintains its infrastructure and operates its trains, but also manufactures its rolling stock. There are six production units in Indian Railway, which are:

- Chittaranjan Locomotive Works at Chittaranjan which manufactures electric locomotives.
- Diesel Locomotive Works at Varanasi which manufactures diesel locomotives.
- Integral Coach Factory at Chennai which manufactures passenger coaches.
- Rail Coach factory at Kapurthala.
- Wheel and Axle Plant at Bangalore.
- Diesel Component Works at Patiala which in addition to manufacturing components for diesel locomotives has off late also started rehabilitation of diesel locomotives.

Some new production units are also proposed to be set up such as:

- Forged wheel factory at Rae Bareli in collaboration with Rashtriya Ispat Nigam Ltd.
- Mainline Electrical Multiple Units (MEMU) facility at Bhilwara in Rajasthan in collaboration with Bharat Heavy Electricals Limited (BHEL).
- A coach manufacturing unit in Sonepat, Haryana.
- Locomotive factories at Madhepura and Mahrora in Bihar.
- Wheel factory at Chhapra in Bihar.
- Axle factory at Jalpaiguri in Assam.

- MEMU/DEMU factory at Kancharapara in Bengal.
- A Coach factory in Kerala, etc.

Setting up more and more manufacturing units is announced in the Railway Budget every year.

Manufacture of wagons is entirely in the private sector.

All the production units are fully owned and controlled by the Ministry of Railways. They are captive units producing only for Indian Railways, though some locomotives have been exported to Bangladesh, Thailand and South Africa. Indian Railways is self-sufficient with respect to rolling stock. Some higher capacity locomotives have been imported in the past.

All production units are headed by a General Manager reporting directly to the Member Mechanical in the Railway Board except for the General Manager of Chittaranjan Locomotive Works who reports to the Member Electrical. The middle and senior management personnel are drawn from the open line cadre of Indian Railways who revert to the open line after a few years. Thus, the personnel in the production units and open line are interchangeable except for the employees up to the senior supervisory level.

Being a part of Indian Railways acts as a hindrance to the realisation of the full potential of the production units.

IR is the single owner and single customer of the production units. The production units produce only what is required by Indian Railways. Indian Railways meets the entire cost of manufacture. Therefore, there is neither the necessity nor the incentive to innovate, improve productivity or reduce costs. The production units are in the same situation as and suffer from the same smugness as the automobile industry suffered before it was opened to competition.

Since its middle and senior management personnel are interchangeable with open line, they are more of generalist engineers than production engineers. The same engineers are expected to be experts in maintenance and operation of assets while working in the open line and experts in production technology while working in the production units. The resultant compromise in professionalism needs no further elaboration. It is well recognised that manufacturing is a specialised field requiring specialised skills. Hence, it should be entrusted to such specialists only.

Same applies to other branches in the production units such as Finance and Personnel. The personnel problems in the workshops and manufacturing units are entirely different from those in the open line. So are the expectations from the finance and accounts department. A finance officer in a manufacturing organisation ought to be a costing expert, while a finance officer in an open line position need not be so.

Interchange of personnel between open line and production units has another unintended effect. The persons posted to the production units, naturally, see themselves as essentially birds of passage and look for their career prospects in the open line rather than in the production units. This in no way implies their less than total commitment to the 'job at hand'. But it would be unreasonable to expect from them as much long-term commitment as from persons who see their future in the production unit itself.

Many experts have repeatedly recommended shedding off the manufacturing facilities in railways.

This is eminently desirable and can be done without affecting railway operations in any way. In fact, it will be beneficial both for railways and for the production units. It must be done without any delay.

Broad contours of such a set-up are described below.

- Ideally all the production units should be put under a holding company as a separate public sector undertaking which may be called Indian Railway Manufacturing Corporation (IRMC), with each production unit having a good degree of independence. However, since under the current rules, a public sector undertaking has to be under the administrative control of some Ministry of the Government of India, there can be no other Ministry better than the Ministry of Railways to administer this public sector undertaking. After all, it is only the Ministry of Railways which understands railways better than anyone else and can provide back-up support, as and when needed. Putting it under any other Ministry such as the Ministry of Heavy Industry, for example, would be a mistake. In this context it needs to be noted that unlike the undertakings under other ministries, the Ministry of Railways is the only one whose undertakings have consistently performed well and earned profit.

  But a mechanism has also to be found to ensure that the control of the Ministry of Railways on the holding company of the production units is minimal.
- To start with, the proposed holding company may be a fully government-owned company. But its ownership should be gradually

diluted up to 49 per cent to be passed on to private hands, in order to reduce the stronghold of the Ministry of Railways. The fund generated by dilution of equity can be used by the company to – i) pay off part of the capital invested by the Government of India in the production units to become a debt-free company and ii) on research and development. A complete privatisation is neither necessary nor visualised in the near future.

- The new company should have a global vision. This implies that the company will not be a captive company of Indian Railways. Indian Railways will be only one of its customers. The world should be its market. International competition will necessarily compel it to undertake intensive research and development to enable it to survive. This will also benefit Indian Railways.
- Similarly, for Indian Railways too this company will be only one of its suppliers. It will be free to procure its rolling stock from any internal or external source based on quality and cost.
- It should have its own cadre specialised in manufacturing technology. Its Directors should be selected by the Public Enterprises Selection Board from applicants from railways, public sector and the private sector as in the case of other Public Sector Undertakings.
- The Board of the Holding Company should have Independent Director from outside the Railways.
- During the interim period when its shares are not divested, the company will have to necessarily depend upon financial support from Indian Railways. But in due course it will have to be responsible for raising its own resources like any other commercial enterprise.
- The company should be accorded all the powers and flexibility required for it to survive and prosper in a competitive commercial environment both within the country and outside.
- In due course, a suitable compensation and incentive policy may need to be drawn up to attract best talent to the company.
- The company should have three fields of activity
  - Manufacture and sale of locomotives, coaches, wheels and axles etc.
  - Reconditioning or refurbishing of rolling stock.
  - Supply of locomotives, coaches, wheel sets and axles etc. to other Railways on sale or lease.

Sale and lease of locomotives to railways outside India, is presently the responsibility of Rites and IRCON. This may continue to remain with them because of their vast experience in marketing and their already existing wide international network.

It can be reasonably expected that such a company, free from the shackles of government rules and procedures and faced with international competition will be forced to carry out research, innovate, be more productive and reduce costs. In the long run, both Indian Railways and the production units will benefit from it.

15

Rounding Up

Purely in terms of antiquity the realisation of need for change in railway business and the direction of change in Indian Railways predate reforms in other railways. Though railways in India started in the 1850s as a commercial venture, it lost this character over a period of time. The Acworth Committee (1921) tried to revive it by emphasising the 'essentially commercial' nature of Indian Railways. But not much has been done to put it in practice. This was followed by some powerful Committees after independence which talked of corporatizing Railways.

According to the Wanchoo Committee on Railway Accidents (1968),

> A more radical and fundamental method of eliminating political influence in such matters may be to **convert the Railway Board into an autonomous statutory corporation.**

This was followed by the Administrative Reforms Committee in 1970.

> **If the constitution of the Railways into a statutory corporation in the present context is not considered feasible ...**

The Railway Reforms Committee had a different opinion. Its Working Group on Structural Reorganisation (1982) said that

> Considering all aspects of the problem, we have come to the conclusion that ... the **departmental form is the most suited for Indian Railways**.

The Rakesh Mohan Committee (2001) dealt with the subject in greater detail and made some very important recommendations but not adequately enough, most probably because it had a much wider canvas.

However, as usual, nothing much happened.

This book is an attempt to carry the exercise forward. It builds on the recommendations of different experts, adds some more (actually a lot more) to them to develop a holistic structure. Piecemeal approach is unlikely to produce desired results.

The model

Any reform model must meet two criteria. It must be sound as a conceptual construct and also be implementable. The former is not so difficult. The devil lies in the latter. The reform measures proposed in Chapters 10 to 14 are summarised below to give it the form of a holistic structure. This is followed by an evaluation of the model.

There are two main pillars of the reform measures proposed in this book. It is contended that,

- commercialisation of Indian Railways is the only solution
- institutional reform is an essential pre-requisite for the success of any other reform, hence must precede them.

Therefore, this book concentrates on institutional reforms.

The fundamental problem is to accept that railways is a purely commercial undertaking. Without this acceptance, any discussion on reforms is meaningless. Governments in most countries, where reforms have taken place, did accept the essentially commercial nature of railway business, but rather late. Can the Government of India accept it while there is still time?

Once this is accepted the crux of the problem becomes: How to commercialise Indian Railways. This is the central theme of the book. All measures lead only to this single point agenda.

Almost all the proposed measures are interconnected and interdependent. It is difficult to say which should come first. But still one can venture to say that the first step would be to corporatize Indian railways. This is closely connected with separation of three functions relating to Railways – policy making, execution of the policies and regulation. All three are now the preserve of Indian Railways. This confuses Indian Railway's commercial and non-commercial roles. The three functions should be separated. Policy making should be transferred to the Ministry of Transport which would be responsible for coordinated transport policy relating to all modes of transport, rail, road, air and coastal shipping. Execution of the transport policy in respect of railways should be the responsibility of Indian Railways. And the function of regulation of rail transport should be assigned to an independent Rail Regulatory Authority. In such a structure Indian Railways can be conveniently converted into a corporation to be run purely on commercial considerations. This is not to say that railways cannot run services which are not commercially viable. It only implies that those who desire unviable services to be run, should bear its costs rather than railways – user pays principle, as has now become the norm in all the reformed railways.

The relationship between the government, through the Ministry of Transport, and the Indian Railway Corporation, should be governed by a well-defined Memorandum of Undertaking laying down concretised responsibilities of both the government and railways.

An incidental outcome of the MOU scheme would be a reform of more fundamental nature viz. elimination of the need to have a separate Railway Budget, a practice which has been in existence for ninety years. The responsibility for obtaining the sanction of Parliament in respect of railways matters will then shift to the Ministry of Transport. And Railways will be left free to carry out all activities found commercially justifiable without any external influence beyond the terms of the MOU and regulation by the Regulatory Authority.

A contrarian view also exists, mostly within railway circles. It argues for more powers to railways within a government departmental set-up itself. One suspects that this view is most likely the result of inertia and fear of the unknown. It could also arise from apprehensions regarding various disciplines and compulsions which a corporatized Indian Railways will be compelled to impose on all aspects of railway working.

But corporatisation alone will not make railways a commercial undertaking. A lot many supporting steps will have to be taken to make commercialisation effective, such as creating appropriate organisational and financial structures, commercial orientation in the minds of railway men, providing powers, freedom and flexibility to railways as normally available to any commercial enterprise etc. These will necessarily involve borrowing some principles and practices from the commercial world.

Beginning must be made with the structure at the very top, i.e., the Railway Board itself. Two steps are required to impart commercial orientation to the Board – creating a post of Member Commercial and inducting some Members from outside railways. Two Members from the banking sector viz. one from the largest public sector bank and one from the largest private sector bank and three representatives one each from the three organised associations of industry should be inducted into the Board.

With the creation of the post of Member Commercial and induction of five Independent Members the size of the Railway Board will increase from seven to thirteen. At present, the Board meets almost once a week. With increase in the size of the Board and the induction of independent Members who may not be able to spare much time, it would neither be necessary nor practicable to have such frequent meetings of the Board. Therefore, there should be a two-tier Board – one consisting only of the functional Members which may meet frequently and the other the full Board which may meet when necessary, at least as per the requirement of the Companies Act.

Further, the Board should be strengthening by vesting it with all the decision-making powers now exercised by the Government in respect of investments, expansion, curtailing or discontinuing services, fixation of tariffs (subject to the Regulatory Authority's approval), appointments and promotions to higher management posts etc. The role of the government should be the minimum.

One of the biggest problems in Indian Railways is lack of professionalism in its manning policies. This is reflected in four of its practices:

- The manner of selection of officials for manning such critically important posts as those of Divisional Railway Managers, General Managers of zonal railways and the Chairman Railway Board
- Posting of Member Staff
- Eligibility criteria for the selection of Class 1 officers of the non-technical departments and
- The shortness of tenures of Chairman and Members of the Railway Board.

The present philosophy presumes that all railway officers *ipso facto* are endowed with the qualities and skills required for the posts of Divisional Railway Managers, General Managers, Chairman Railway Board, Member Staff etc. As a result, any officer belonging to any department senior enough and competent enough (based on a highly debatable document called Confidential Reports) can be posted on these posts. The consequence of this practice needs no elaboration. It is vitally important that this practice be given up as soon as possible. It has, therefore, been suggested that a separate management cadre

Indian Railway Executive Services (IRES) should be created from amongst all railway officers of middle management level by selecting persons possessing proper aptitude. They should then be imparted training suitable for manning these posts in a commercial environment. Only the persons belonging to the management cadre should be posted to the higher administrative posts.

It has also been suggested that the selection for the posts of General Managers and the Chairman Railway Board should be conducted by an independent body viz. the Union Public Service Commission or the Public Enterprises Selection Board. Similarly, selection for the post of other Members of the Board should also be conducted by the UPSC or the PESB.

Two more objectives are sought to be achieved by creation of the management cadre and selection for senior positions through the UPSC/PESB – achieving primacy of merit over seniority and minimisation, if not complete elimination, of scope for biases and prejudices in selection for these posts. This is done at two stages. First is the stage when selection is made for initial entry into the Indian Railway Executive Service at the level of Additional Divisional Railway Managers. Second stage is selection for the very senior positions through an independent selection agency. This will ensure that only really meritorious persons occupy these positions and leave little scope for influence by an external agency.

As regards the post of Member Staff, it is difficult to explain why this post is not filled by a person from the Indian Railway Personnel Service in spite of such a service being in existence for more than 35 years. At present, it is manned by a person from any of the railway services. There cannot be a better example of ad-hocism.

Another unexplainable lack of professionalism is the eligibility criteria for the selection of Class 1 officers of the non-technical departments such as the Indian Railway Accounts Service, Indian Railway Personnel Service, Indian Railway Traffic Service and Indian Railway Stores Service. Eligibility criterion for selection to the technical services in railways is being a graduate in engineering. On the other hand, for the first three of the above-mentioned services a graduate in any subject including History, Hindi, Sanskrit, Urdu, Persian and what have you is eligible to be selected. In case of the Stores Service, persons who appear and qualify for the engineering service but do not meet the vision criteria are offered a post in the Stores department. Now that candidates with relevant professional qualification are available in abundance, this practice should be given up. Only persons professionally qualified in relevant fields should be eligible to appear for those services.

One of the most important factors militating against commercial orientation in Railways is the historical primacy of the operating function and the culture flowing from it. The entire thinking is geared towards physical parameters only to the complete disregard of the financial factors – revenue, cost and profits. This is not in consonance with commercial culture. The problem will get partially mitigated by creating the post of Member Commercial, but only partly.

The surest way of inculcating commercial orientation is to create a stake of all concerned, from the lowest employee to the highest, in the financial success of the organisation. This can be achieved through a well-designed incentive scheme. The existing incentive scheme in the form of Productivity Linked Bonus (PLB) scheme takes into account only the physical performance of railways. It is, therefore, totally incapable of creating any motivation for improving railway finances. Actually the existing PLB scheme suffers from many structural flaws. Its structural deficiency becomes clear from the fact that if extrapolated logically it might lead to a situation where Bonus will have to be paid even if railway is in loss. This PLB scheme must, therefore, be replaced with a well-crafted incentive scheme which takes into account physical as well as financial performance. The outlines of such a scheme have been described in the book. The proposed scheme has the added feature of covering all employees from the lowest to the highest and establishing more visible and direct relationship between performance and reward.

A long-standing contentious issue between the Government and Railways has been the loss suffered by Railways on carrying out activities which are normally the responsibility of the Government. Railways have long been demanding from the Government compensation for such losses. The Railway Convention Committee 1998 also unequivocally recommended such compensation. However, it has not yet been accepted by the Government. This is indefensible even at present, more so in a commercial environment.

Another anomaly is the capital structure of the Railways. It consists entirely of non-repayable debt from the Government of India. This is not in keeping with the normal capital structure of a commercial enterprise which consists of both debt and equity. It has multidimensional harmful effects. It has, therefore, been suggested that the existing Capital-at Charge should be converted into Government's equity in Railways. However, all future funds from the Government should be in the form of repayable debt on commercial terms. This will eventually lead to a balance between debt and equity in the capital structure of Railways.

No doubt the suggestion of repayable debt on commercial terms will cast some financial burden on railways having impact on tariffs. One way of reducing the impact would be subsidy from the government. Even in such a situation the subsidy from the government should be in the form of specific subsidy not in the form of concessional interest rate or some such method.

Creating an Indian Railway Corporation (IRC) and converting railway's debt from the government into equity should be taken a step further. IRC should be listed with the stock exchange and a part of its shares should be gradually off-loaded into the market. This will not only provide railways with much needed funds for improvement and growth, it will also relieve the Government from the necessity of providing funds to railways. The savings so made can be used for other development or social welfare work. Additional benefit of divesting of shares into the market will be that the pressures of the stock market will force railways to perform better.

Another much desirable financial reform would be to convert the Divisions into business units. At present, the smallest business unit is a railway zone in the sense that it is the smallest unit for which financial statements are separately prepared and profitability separately calculated. But a railway zone is too large a unit for effective financial management. Better financial management can be achieved by reducing the size of the business unit to Divisions. This does not mean that all Divisions have, necessarily, to be profitable. Some Divisions are by location or traffic mix prone to be loss making. In their case also preparation of separate financial statements will enable at least better management of its costs.

Shedding off the non-core activities by Indian Railways is often talked about. And the activities most frequently identified for shedding off/privatisation are – production units, health, education, catering, retiring rooms, colony maintenance and construction. Production units, education, catering and retiring rooms can certainly be shed off. The situation is not so clear about colony maintenance and construction. But it would be totally imprudent to shed off the medical facilities. It will not only lead to grave employee dissatisfaction, it will also be a much more expensive proposition for railways.

Production units are in a different league altogether. They not only should, but must be shed off. Hiving off the production units will in no way affect the operational working of railways. On the other hand, being captive units of railways producing only for Indian Railways according to the technical requirements of Indian Railways on a cost-plus basis has stymied the growth of rolling stock manufacturing capability in the country technically as well as capacity-wise. There is no incentive to innovate or economise. Therefore, the production units should be separated from Indian Railways and organised into a separate holding company. And the market for the rolling stock holding company should not Indian Railways only but the whole world. Like the Indian Railway Corporation, it too should be listed with the stock exchange and a part of its shares should be gradually divested. This will enable the company to generate funds for expansion, research and innovation.

A critique of the model

The conceptual construct of the model has been described above. It simultaneously raises a lot of questions. Clear cut answers are difficult. What can be provided is only logical deduction. Some of the important questions which arise are as follows.

The model requires the government to forego not only its control over Railways and a fixed annual income from Railways by way of Dividend but requires the government to pay for the cost of Public Service Obligations which is at present around ₹ 20,000 Crs. per annum. The question is what does the government get in return?

- At first sight it appears that in financial terms, the government will not get much. It will only get a share of Dividend calculated on the basis of commercial principles which may not be much, if at all. This impression is partially correct. But what must also be taken into account is that the government will be saved of the obligation to finance railway investments. This saving will more than offset the loss of fixed Dividend as the loan from government to railways is always more than the Dividend paid by Railways. During the year 2011–12 funds provided by the government to Railways was ₹ 18,227 Crs. while the Dividend paid by Railways was ₹ 5,656 Crs. Thus, in total the government paid ₹ 12,571 Crs to Railways which it would have saved if railways had to find this resource from some other source or obtain this as loan from the government on commercial terms. The funds so released can be used by the government for other purposes.
- The government will also benefit financially from additional taxes which it would collect on increased economic activity as a result of expanded railway network and improved services. But then, this cannot be quantified even very grossly. It will depend on the extent of economic activity that gets promoted which will in turn depend upon

a host of other factors such as government policies, other infrastructural facilities, demand and so on. However, the possibility of such additional revenue to the Government cannot be totally ignored.

Payment for the cost of Public Service Obligations is another issue. It is correct that the government will have to pay quite a substantial amount to railways on this account. But this must be looked at from a different angle. The cost is in any case being incurred. It is only that the cost is being borne by Railways on behalf of some other organisation which should actually be responsible for it. It is thus only a question of proper allocation of costs and not incurrence of additional cost. The payment for such costs by the concerned Ministries will enable costs to be allocated where they should actually pertain. Proper allocation of costs will enable better understanding of the true cost of such services or facilities. This will in turn lead to more rational allocation of resources by the government. Simultaneously, it will also provide more funds to Railways which can be used for improvements and development. Not to mention the healthy impact that it will have on the image of Railways.

Another important but ticklish question which arises is: The relationship between the government and the railways is expected to be only through a MOU which is of the nature of a contract. What happens if any party fails to perform according to the MOU? If the government fails to honour its commitments, it will naturally have an impact on the performance of Railways. It may even lead to financial loss and entitle Railways for compensation. What happens if Railways fail to honour its part of the MOU? Can the government claim damages? If so, what impact will it have on the financial condition of Railways? Or conversely what happens if Railways perform better than the MOU parameters? Should it be rewarded as an incentive? There are no straight answers. They will require framing of detailed contractual conditions and be better left to the framers of the MOU and the Rail Regulatory Authority.

Another question which arises is: How to ensure that railways expand or upgrade its network according to the needs of the economy or as desired by the government on social considerations. This is rather easy to answer. The obvious mechanism is the MOU.

There are three factors that may affect the success of the above model or for that matter any model for the reform of railways.

(a) The biggest problem will arise from its acceptability by the labour unions. And no reform measure can succeed without the cooperation of the unions. The unions will find it unacceptable on two a counts – rationalisation of staff which would be unavoidable and modification of the incentive scheme. Railways will find it impossibly difficult to rationalise its labour force estimated to have at least 25 per cent surplus staff, i.e., about 3 lakh staff. By all stretch of imagination, this is mind boggling and cannot be handled by Railways on its own. The government will have to somehow step in as has been done in all other countries. The success of any attempt to make Indian Railways an efficient and productive railway will hinge on successful handling of its labour question.

(b) The next imponderable is that the model places heavy reliance on the ability of Railways to raise resources for investment purposes on its own. A little explanation will narrow down the problem. The problem can be broken down into three parts. As far as unviable projects are concerned, it is expected that in a commercial environment the government will bear the costs for such projects and services. And the commercially viable 'bankable' projects can be financed through internal resources of Railways as well as repayable loan from banks or the government on commercial terms. Thirdly, divesting of shares, in due course, will also bring in quite substantial investible funds. Thus, reliance on government funding of investments is avoidable except perhaps in the form of sovereign guarantee in the case of loan from multilateral funding agencies.

(c) Another difficult problem to tackle would be the non-commercial culture of railways solidified over almost a century. It will be almost a Herculean task to mould it to commercial orientation – to think in terms of revenue, costs and profit. The model proposes to do it in four ways. One is emphasising the commercial nature of the organisation by creating a separate post of Member Commercial. But this in itself will not amount to much. A more potent instrument would be the implementation of an incentive scheme which lays equal emphasis on physical as well as financial performance of railways and creates financial stake of all employees, from the lowest to the highest, in its financial success. The third factor which is expected to have an impact on commercial orientation in Railways would be the presence of eminent persons from industry and the financial sector as independent Members in the Board. But it would be impractical to entertain any illusion that commercial orientation in Indian Railways can be created in a hurry. The fourth, but more potent, factor will be the fear of dishonouring of cheques by banks for want of balance once Indian railways is converted into a corporation.

(d) No reform is possible without a lot of sacrifices and surrenders – willingly or unwillingly. The political class will have to surrender vast opportunities for power, pelf and patronage – amounting to almost saint-like self-denial. Similar is the case of the role of the government bureaucracy including the Planning Commission and their sanctioning powers. The railway management needs to do away with its complacency, status quoism and the seniority syndrome. So must organised labour. It will have to surrender its indifference to the finances of the organisation. But the most difficult to surrender is the surrender of 'attitudes' all around.

Even individually these 'surrenders' are quite formidable. Taken together, they add up to almost the proverbial immovable object. But reforms which do not call for sacrifices and surrenders are no reforms at all. They are placebos.

Thus, there are quite some imponderables and major hurdles as in the case of any socio-economic reform model. It would not be an easy and painless passage. But that is in the nature of reforms. Crisis also begets courage. In the case of Indian Railways the crisis has existed for quite some time. It is the willingness and courage to change which have been missing.

In India as elsewhere, it is the political class alone which is capable of pushing through reforms of this magnitude. Reforms in Indian Railways will, therefore, depend entirely on when the political leaders are able to realise its inevitability and urgency and gather enough courage to undertake it.

16

The Road Ahead

Logically, any reform process is composed of six elements viz. – realisation that reform is necessary, willingness and courage to change, structuring the change, implementation, evaluation and course correction. This book deals only with the third element, i.e., structuring the change which is perhaps the easiest of all. The most difficult being the 'willingness and courage to change'. Once the willingness and courage to change is picked up, the rest can easily follow.

Although many reform measures have been discussed in this book, the first action required on the part of the government would be to set up a committee to examine this issue in detail and recommend appropriate reforms required in Indian Railways.

This chapter attempts to frame a likely time schedule for implementing the reforms suggested in this book just to give an idea of the process involved. Obviously, the actual stages and time frame will depend upon the recommendations of the committee.

After the committee submits its recommendation, there will be the need to set up a high-powered independent authority to examine the recommendations of the committee and take all actions necessary to implement the recommendations found acceptable.

Preparation (Period 1 year 6 months)

- Appoint a high-powered authority to concretise and implement reforms.
- Bring management and organised labour on board.
- Obtain in-principle approval of the government.
- Prepare a stage-wise action plan.

- Identify and prepare the legal documents.
- Obtain Parliament's sanction for amendment of the Indian Railway Act, and Act for the creation of Indian Railway Corporation and other legal measures.
- Prepare education documents.
- Undertake education drive at all levels.

Stage 1 (Period 1 year)

- Separate Policy, Execution and Regulation.
- Corporatise – set up Indian Railway Corporation.
- Set up Rail Regulatory Authority.
- Expanded Railway Board.
- MOU with the government.
- Implement a new Incentive Scheme.
- Increase tenures of senior management positions.

Review (Period 3 months)

- Consolidate
- Review
- Modify

Stage 2 (Period 6 months)

- Set up Indian Railway Executive Service.
- Implement revised selection procedure for senior positions.
- Discontinue recruitment to Special Class Railway Apprentice.
- Implement professional qualifications for non-technical services.
- Implement division as a business unit.
- Shed off education, catering and retiring rooms.

Review (Period 3 months)

- Consolidate
- Review
- Modify

Stage 3 (Period 6 months)

- List Indian Railway Corporation in stock exchange.
- Set up Indian Railway Manufacturing Corporation (IRMC) for production Units.
- Partially off-load shares in Indian Railway Corporation.

Review (Period 3 months)

- Consolidate
- Review
- Modify

Stage 4 (Period 1 year)

- Enlist Indian Railway Manufacturing Corporation (IRMC) in stock exchange.
- Partially off-load share in IRMC.

Review (Period 3 months)

- Consolidate
- Review
- Modify

Once major part of the reform process is completed, the authority set up to implement the reform measures should be wound up. It is difficult to say when the 'major' part of the reform process can be said to have been completed, because reform is a continuous process. However, after the shares of the holding company of production units are partially shed off, the reform process can be said to have picked up momentum and the independent authority can be wound up. The remaining process may be completed by the Board of the Corporation.

The total time period for various stages and reviews indicated above adds up to five years and six months. But this in no way indicates the time required for the total reform process to be completed. It may be shortened by conducting some activities in parallel. It may also get delayed because of the unforeseen problems. Time required will vary depending upon a host of factors, such as the quality and number of manpower deployed, time taken in bringing the management and labour on board, time taken by government agencies, time taken in the completion of legal formalities etc.

The above stages do not form any water-tight compartmentalisation either. Some activities may overlap and overflow from one stage to the other. The stages merely indicate the sequence of different items of work to be undertaken.

It would be noticed that the maximum time has been shown against 'Preparation'. This is very important. Indian projects often suffer from the fault of spending too little time and effort in planning and preparation. Time spent in preparation saves time spent in implementation. Importance of planning the minutest detail and preparation cannot be over-emphasised.

It will also be noticed that a review has been proposed after every stage. This again is extremely important. The task is huge and complex. Unforeseen problems are bound to arise. Therefore, a period must be allowed to cool down, absorb and consolidate so that the unforeseen problems come to the foreground and are resolved. They might well require modifications to steps already taken, institutions set up and procedures established. But one thing is sure. It should not be hurried. For an organisation like Indian Railways, it would not be surprising if the process takes a even a decade.

Annexure

A Note on Leasing through IRFC and Dividend Payment

> 'The expert study in question was undertaken by Jawaharlal Nehru University at the instance of Railway Capital Restructuring Committee (RCRC1995). It concluded that even allowing for the obligation to pay Dividend in perpetuity on capital provided by the Government, this funding option was definitely cheaper than the leasing arrangement through IRFC.'
>
> Rakesh Mohan Committee Report

The above statement needs to be extended further. The main conditions in case of loan from IRFC are as follows. The lease charges realised by IRFC from railways consist of three elements – rate of interest which is the same as the rate paid by IRFC in that particular tranche of loan raised from the market, amortisation charges plus a small administrative charge (0.12 per cent). The lease period is usually 30 years (life of loco for which financing is mainly done). However, the lease charges are so fixed that the entire loan including interest is recovered in 15 years. During the period 2012–13 the lease charges worked out to 8.62 per cent of the loan amount. Thereafter, only nominal lease charges are realised for another 15 years.

In case of loan from the government, Dividend is payable till perpetuity. For the past many years the rate of Dividend has been around 7 per cent or so. For the year 2012–13 the Railway Convention Committee approved a rate of 4 per cent due to the poor financial condition of railways. The Ministry of Finance has been consistently pleading with the railway Convention Committees to raise it to 9 per cent.

The following highly simplified assumptions are made in the example worked out below, though no essential point has been lost.

(i) Loan of ₹ 1000 Crs.
(ii) A rate of interest of 9 per cent has been adopted for calculating NPV. This is normally the rate of interest on longish term deposits with banks. However, the actual rate will make no difference to the conclusions of this analysis as it will have equal effect on all the options. The relative position of the results will not change.
(iii) Project period is 30 years. The period beyond 30 years is irrelevant as the discounting becomes too small irrespective of rate of interest.
(iv) EMI for loan from IRFC at 8.62 per cent of loan
(v) Rate of Dividend 7 per cent
(vi) Earnings, i.e., inflow, of ₹ 100 Crs per annum remains constant throughout.
(vii) No other cost except payment of lease charges or Dividend as outflow, is considered as it will be the same in all cases and thus its effect will cancel out.

In the example given below, NPV of three options are calculated, the NPV of EMIs on loan from IRFC and NPVs of Dividend at three rates – 7 per cent, 8 per cent and 8.6 per cent (which is the same as EMI on IRFC loan). The NPV represents the net benefit to railways at the end of the project period.

It will be seen that at 7 per cent Dividend the option of perpetual paying Dividend on capital-at-Charge is preferable. But the attractiveness of the Dividend paying option goes on reducing as the rate of Dividend is increased. And at 8.6 per cent there is hardly any difference between loan from IRFC and loan from the Government of India except that in the case of the former the cost of the asset will have been fully paid up. It will no more be a part of the Railways Loan Account as in the case of capital-at-charge.

(₹ Crs.)

IRFC Calculations				*Dividend Calculations*					
Year	*Inflow*	*EMI 8.62%*	*Net Cash Flow*	*Rate 7%*	*Net Cash Flow*	*Rate 8%*	*Net Cash Flow*	*Rate 8.6%*	*Net Cash Flow*
1	100	86.2	13.8	70	30	80	20	86	14
2	100	86.2	13.8	70	30	80	20	86	14

Contd.

Contd.

IRFC Calculations				*Dividend Calculations*					
Year	*Inflow*	*EMI 8.62%*	*Net Cash Flow*	*Rate 7%*	*Net Cash Flow*	*Rate 8%*	*Net Cash Flow*	*Rate 8.6%*	*Net Cash Flow*
3	100	86.2	13.8	70	30	80	20	86	14
4	100	86.2	13.8	70	30	80	20	86	14
5	100	86.2	13.8	70	30	80	20	86	14
6	100	86.2	13.8	70	30	80	20	86	14
7	100	86.2	13.8	70	30	80	20	86	14
8	100	86.2	13.8	70	30	80	20	86	14
9	100	86.2	13.8	70	30	80	20	86	14
10	100	86.2	13.8	70	30	80	20	86	14
11	100	86.2	13.8	70	30	80	20	86	14
12	100	86.2	13.8	70	30	80	20	86	14
13	100	86.2	13.8	70	30	80	20	86	14
14	100	86.2	13.8	70	30	80	20	86	14
15	100	86.2	13.8	70	30	80	20	86	14
16	100	0.01	99.9	70	30	80	20	86	14
17	100	0.01	99.99	70	30	80	20	86	14
18	100	0.01	99.99	70	30	80	20	86	14
19	100	0.01	99.99	70	30	80	20	86	14
20	100	0.01	99.99	70	30	80	20	86	14
21	100	0.01	99.99	70	30	80	20	86	14
22	100	0.01	99.99	70	30	80	20	86	14
23	100	0.01	99.99	70	30	80	20	86	14
24	100	0.01	99.99	70	30	80	20	86	14
25	100	0.01	99.99	70	30	80	20	86	14
26	100	0.01	99.99	70	30	80	20	86	14
27	100	0.01	99.99	70	30	80	20	86	14
28	100	0.01	99.99	70	30	80	20	86	14
29	100	0.01	99.99	70	30	80	20	86	14
30	100	0.01	99.99	70	30	80	20	86	14
NPV			₹ 1.53		₹ 3.33		₹ 2.22		₹ 1.56

Source: Compiled by author

Select Bibliography

1. *Acworth Committee Report*, 1921.
2. Andrea Obermauer, 'National Railway Reform in Japan and the EU: Evaluation of Institutional Changes', *Japan Railway & Transport Review*, 29 December 2001.
3. Andrei Dementiev, 'Vertical Divestiture as a Competitive Strategy: The Case of Russian Railway Reform', 4th Annual Conference on 'Railroad Industry Structure, Competition and Investment' Universidad Carlos III de Madrid, Spain, October 2006.
4. Arpita Mukherjee and Richika Sachdeva, 'Trend in Land Transport Services', Working Paper No. 13, January 2004, The Indian Council for Research on International Economic Relations, New Delhi.
5. Dan Bogart And Latika Chaudhury, 'Engine of Growth: The Productivity Advance of Indian Railways 1874–1912, University of California, Berkley, October 2011.
6. Dan Bogart And Latika Chaudhury, 'Railways in Colonial India: An Economic Achievement, August 2011.
7. David Bringshaw, 'China Takes the First Step Towards Reform', *International Railway Journal*, April 2013.
8. Expert Group on Indian Railways, 'The Indian Railway Report: Policy Imperatives for Reinvention and Growth', National Council of Applied Economic Research, India, 2001.
9. Fumitoshi Mizutani and Kiyoshi Nakumara, 'The Japanese Experience with Railway Restructuring', Governance, Regulation and Privatisation in Asia-Pacific Region, NBER East Asia Seminar on Economics, Vol. 12, University of Chicago Press, January 2004.
10. G. Alexandersson and S. Hulten, 'The Swedish Railway Deregulation Path', *Review of Network Economics*, Vol. 7, 1 March 2008.
11. G. Huddleston, *History of East Indian Railway* 1906.

12. Gerard Mathieu, 'The Reform of UK Railways – Privatisation and its Results' *Japan railway & Transport Review No. 34.*
13. Heike Link, 'Restructuring Railways: German Railway Reform – Chances and Risks', *Japan Railway and Transport Review No. 2.*
14. Hisako Tsuji and Dmitry L. Sergachev, 'An Overview of Russian Railways: Current Reforms and Expansion in the Far Eastern Region (Summary)', *ERINA Report* Vol. 62, March 2005.
15. Indian Railway Budget Documents 2013–14.
16. Indian Railway Convention Committee Reports for various years.
17. *Indian Railway Year Book, 2012.*
18. Jan-Eric Nilsson, 'Restructuring Swedish Railway System: The Unintentional Deregulation', Swedish National Road and Transport Research Institute, 2003.
19. Jian Wong Wu and Chris Nash, 'Railway Reform in China', Institute of Transport Studies, University of Leeds, Working Paper No. 524, 1998.
20. Jose A. Gomez-Ibanez, 'Railroad Reform: An Overview of Options', Conference on Railway Reform, Rafel del Pino Foundation, Madrid, September 2004.
21. K. B. Verma, 'In Pursuit of a Productive Relationship', *Readings in Indian Railway Finance*, Academic Foundation, India, 1998.
22. Louis S. Thompson, Hennie Deboeck and Richard Speo, 'Railway Reforms in China: The Great Railway Challenge', World Bank, 2004.
23. Louis S. Thompson, 'Privatising British Railways: Are There Lessons for World Bank and its Borrowers, World Bank, 2004.
24. M. Q. Dalvi, 'Should Indian Railways Be Privatised', *Readings in Indian Railway Finance*, ed. K. B. Verma, Academic Foundation, India, 1998.
25. Ministry of Railways, 'Explanatory Memorandum to Railway Budget 2013–14'.
26. Ministry of Railways, *Railway Fare and Freight Committee Report, India*, 1993.
27. Ministry of Railways, *Report of the Expert group for Modernisation of Indian Railways*, February 2012.
28. Neil Clarke, 'The Public Wants Railway Nationalised – What Are We Waiting For?', *The Guardian*, 4 October 2012.
29. Peter Hafner, 'The Effects of Railroad Reform in Germany', *Japan Railway & Transport Review*, September 1996.
30. Qi Zongxi and Yang Jiaxiang 'China implements radical railway reforms', IRJ, 2 August 2013.
31. Ron Kopiciki and Louis S. Thomson, 'Best Methods of Railway Restructuring and Privatisation', *World Bank CFS Discussion Paper Series*, Number 111.
32. Russell Pittman, 'Blame the Switchman ? Russian Railways Restructuring After Ten Years', Economic Analysis Group, Discussion Paper, U.S. Department of Justice, February 2011.

33. Russell Pittman, 'Russian Railways Reform and The Problem of non-discriminatory Access to Infrastructure', *Annals of Public and Cooperative Economics*, 2004, 167–192.
34. Staffen Hulten, 'Opening Up the Pandora Box of Deregulation – The Deregulation Process of Swedish Railway System', Stockholm School of Economics.
35. Tatsuhiko Suga, 20 Years After JNR Privatisation: A Bird's-Eye View of World Railway Reform Trends', *Japan Railway & Transport Review No. 47.*
36. Vishwas R. Udrigar, 'India: Railway Sector Investment Program', Pricewaterhouse Coopers(P) Ltd., India, *ADB Report*, November 2008.

Index

About the Author

K. B. Verma is a retired officer of Indian Railway Accounts Service. He has worked in various capacities in the Finance Department of Indian Railways as well as ADRM in a large railway Division. He has held courses on railway finance for four years in the National Academy of Indian Railways, Vadodara. He worked for five years in Zambia Railways and did a consultancy assignment in Swaziland Railways. He also worked for seven years in Rites, finally retiring as Director Finance of IRCON. His noteworthy publications include: *An Alternative Approach to Capital Productivity and Resource Allocation on Indian Railways* (1996) and *Readings in Indian Railway Finance* (1998).